Aunt Bee's MAYBERRY COOKBOOK

KEN BECK *and* JIM CLARK

RECIPES EDITED BY JULIA M. PITKIN

HARPER
HORIZON

Dedicated to the memory of Frances Bavier

Recipes, additional material, and compilation © 1991 Ken Beck and Jim Clark

The Andy Griffith Show and all elements thereof © 1991 Mayberry Enterprises, Inc.

Published by Harper Horizon, an imprint of HarperCollins Focus LLC.

Any internet addresses, phone numbers, or company or product information printed in this book are offered as a resource and are not intended in any way to be or to imply an endorsement by HarperCollins, nor does HarperCollins vouch for the existence, content, or services of these sites, phone numbers, companies, or products beyond the life of this book.

ISBN 978-0-7852-3110-3 (HC)
ISBN 978-0-7852-3111-0 (eBook)

Printed in Italy

20 21 22 23 24   GVI   12 11 10 9 8 7 6 5 4 3

Contents

The Andy Griffith Show

Cast

Andy Griffith—Andy Taylor
Don Knotts—Barney Fife
Ron Howard—Opie Taylor
Frances Bavier—Aunt Bee Taylor
Howard McNear—Floyd Lawson
Hal Smith—Otis Campbell
Betty Lynn—Thelma Lou
Aneta Corsaut—Helen Crump
Jim Nabors—Gomer Pyle
George Lindsey—Goober Pyle
Jack Dodson—Howard Sprague
Paul Hartman—Emmett Clark
Jack Burns—Warren Ferguson
Hope Summers—Clara Edwards Johnson
Denver Pyle—Briscoe Darling
Margaret Ann Peterson—Charlene Darling
Doug Dillard, Rodney Dillard, Dean Webb,
    Mitch Jayne—The Darling Boys
Howard Morris—Ernest T. Bass
Elinor Donahue—Ellie Walker
Jack Prince—Rafe Hollister
Dick Elliott—Mayor Pike
Parley Baer—Mayor Roy Stoner
Cheerio Meredith—Emma (Watson) Brand
Clint Howard—Leon
Joyce Jameson—Fun Girl Skippy
Jean Carson—Fun Girl Daphne
Ken Berry—Sam Jones
Arlene Golonka—Millie Hutchins
Dennis Rush—Howie Pruitt/Williams
Richard Keith (Keith Thibodeaux)—Johnny
    Paul Jason
James Best—Jim Lindsay
Bernard Fox—Malcolm Merriweather
Joanna Moore—Peggy McMillan
Sheldon (Golomb) Collins—Arnold Bailey
Charles P. Thompson—Asa Breeney

Production Crew

Mayberry Enterprises—production company
Sheldon Leonard—executive producer
Richard O. Linke—associate producer
Aaron Ruben—producer and director
Bob Ross—producer and director
Bob Sweeney—director
Coby Ruskin—director
Alan Rafkin—director
Lee Philips—director
Earle Hagen—music director
Lee Greenway—makeup
Frank E. Myers—production manager
Ronald Jacobs—production supervisor
Sid Hickox—director of photography
Ruth Burch—casting

Core Writers

Arthur Stander
David Adler
Jim Fritzell and Everett Greenbaum
Harvey Bullock and Ray Saffian Allen
Jack Elinson and Charles Stewart
Bill Idelson and Sam Bobrick
Fred S. Fox
Fred Freeman and Lawrence J. Cohen
John Whedon
Ben Joelson and Art Baer
Ben Gershman and Leo Soloman
Dick Bensfield and Perry Grant
Michael Morris and Seaman Jacobs
Aaron Ruben
Bob Ross

Introduction

Mayberry, with just a wink and a nod, almost seems like a real place. Certainly, no one epitomizes the homespun love in Mayberry better than Aunt Bee. And no one puts more love into a meal than she does.

We can almost smell the pot roast simmering in Aunt Bee's oven or the coffee brewing on the stove. We can practically taste her freshly baked apple or butterscotch pecan pies right through our television sets.

In compiling this cookbook, we have tried to capture and preserve the same kind of warmth and love that Aunt Bee has when she prepares a meal for Andy and Opie and her guests.

Just as Aunt Bee would have done, we had a great deal of help from our friends (see Acknowledgments). There is a strong emphasis on Southern cooking because that's what Aunt Bee knows best. But Aunt Bee has traveled to Mexico and has had her own Chinese restaurant, so more exotic foods have their place in this cookbook, too. And goodness knows that Aunt Bee's pickles are well traveled, so you'll be pickled tink to find several variations of "kerosene cucumbers."

This cookbook is also written with an awareness that not everybody in Mayberry cooks. So in addition to the more than three hundred recipes, we've also stirred in dialogue from *The Andy Griffith Show*, plus assorted tidbits of food trivia pertaining to Mayberry. Our goal is that the fun of reading this book in your den will match its usefulness in your kitchen.

We hope you enjoy all the recipes in *Aunt Bee's Mayberry Cookbook*, and we welcome your feedback. Meanwhile, may you and yours have a good time preparing and eating some spectacular dishes!

—Ken Beck and Jim Clark

Aunt Bee Taylor

Aunt Bee

Aunt Bee Taylor is one of the all-time greats in the kitchen. Her nephew Sheriff Andy Taylor admits that when it comes to cooking, "Aunt Bee's got a green thumb." And his son Opie says, "She's the best cook in Mayberry."

Perhaps the greatest proof of her talent is that the only time the Darling Boys were ever heard to talk was after eating one of her satisfying suppers. One of the boys said, "Great beans, Aunt Bee," while another was overheard remarking, "About to pop."

Of course, in response to such high praise, Aunt Bee will usually say, "Oh, fiddle-faddle" or "flibbertigibbet!" Still, deep down she appreciates the warm compliments of her loved ones and fellow Mayberrians.

If any two people know Aunt Bee's talents with food, they're Andy and Opie. After all, Aunt Bee has practically raised both of them on her good home cooking. And although his physique doesn't show it, wiry Deputy Barney Fife has also been on the receiving end of many of Aunt Bee's sumptuous meals.

Beatrice ("she who makes happy" in Latin) Taylor was born in West Virginia and raised in Morgantown. Her family moved to Peoria when she was eighteen. She has sisters named Florence, Ellen, and Nora.

Although she never married, Bee is an outstanding homemaker. Opie can rest assured the cookie jar is never empty and that there will always be plenty of milk on hand to wash the cookies down.

There's no better way to start off a day in Mayberry than with one of Aunt Bee's home-cooked breakfasts topped off with a couple of cups of hot coffee. Her mouthwatering lunches have inspired Andy to call her Miss Luncheon Tray.

But her suppers and desserts are what really make Aunt Bee the queen of Southern country cooking. Among her specialties are such dishes as tunafish casserole, ham loaf with green beans, rib roast, beef casserole, white beans, and potatoes. Most Sundays will see a feast of either fried chicken or roast beef.

Her sweet treats include muffins, chocolate cake, and apple, pecan, Nesselrode, blueberry, and gooseberry pies. She has won blue ribbons at the county fair for her rhubarb pie and homemade strawberry ice cream.

It's no surprise that a cook as wonderful as Aunt Bee can't keep her talents hidden under a bushel basket. She once entertained international palates when a Russian-American summit meeting took place in her house. And she even went Asian when she opened Aunt Bee's Canton Palace, a Chinese restaurant.

Though an unpretentious soul, Aunt Bee has had her moments in the sun. She won the Tampico Tamale Contest with a grand prize of a trip to Mexico. Her knowledge of cooking earned her assorted prizes on the *Win or Lose* game show. Her reputation as a cook also caught the attention of a Siler City television station that signed her up as hostess for its *Mayberry Chef* cooking show.

Bee and best friend Clara were soaring high when their "My Hometown" song was recorded by popular singer Keevy Hazelton. But it was Bee who *really* flew when she took to the skies solo in an airplane.

Aunt Bee also sings in the town and church choirs, has worked as secretary in a print shop, and has run for town council. She is a member of the garden club, the Greater Mayberry Historical Society and Tourist Bureau, the women's club, and the civic improvement league. She also enjoys painting with watercolors and knitting.

Of course, nobody's perfect, and with Clara around, Bee always manages to have plenty of time for good old-fashioned gossipin'. Then there's also the little matter of Aunt Bee's homemade pickles and her equally memorable homemade marmalade. She seems to find time for those, too, bless her heart. (Like we said, nobody's perfect.)

What Aunt Bee means most of all to Mayberry is love. Whether it's her delicious cooking, her warm smile, or her caring hugs, nobody brings more heartfelt love to Mayberry than Aunt Bee.

Aunt Bee's
MAYBERRY COOKBOOK

When Aunt Bee's away, Andy and Opie fend for themselves in the kitchen.

ANDY: Your Aunt Bee give us a choice. What'll it be? Chicken or pot roast?

OPIE: How 'bout if we just had some chocolate cookies and milk?

ANDY: No, no. Your Aunt Bee'd skin me alive if she thought I'd give you something like that for supper.

OPIE: But she ain't here.

ANDY: Nope, got to be something more substantial.

OPIE: How about a licorice whip?

ANDY: Naw. You need something that fills you up.

OPIE: We could chew tar. Johnny Paul Jason says tar's real good for the teeth.

ANDY: That's an old wives' tale.

OPIE: Johnny Paul ain't married.

ANDY: Well, it ain't gonna be chocolate cookies and milk and licorice and tar. Now, what'll it be? Chicken or pot roast?

OPIE: Paw, can I have a nickel?

ANDY: Is that for spending or deciding?

OPIE: Deciding.

ANDY: All right. There you are.

OPIE: Paw, is heads chicken or pot roast?

ANDY: Pot roast.

OPIE: Then we're having chicken.

ANDY: Now let's see, according to Aunt Bee's list . . . Wait . . . give me my nickel.

Menus

Planning the meals you serve should be an entertaining experience. Here are a few suggestions for menus filled with the flavor of Mayberry. They're intended to be merely a starting point for menu ideas. We hope you'll have fun designing menus of your own by using many of the delicious recipes in this cookbook.

Rising Sun Breakfast
Orange Juice and Coffee
Myrtle's Melon Balls
Grandma's Biscuits
Gomer's Banana Bread Pyle
Betty's Breakfast Grits Casserole
or Hash Browns Helen
Mr. McBeevee's Make-Ahead Breakfast

Bee's Brunch
Aunt Rebecca's Salad
Spinach Salad Sprague
Bran Muffins Moulage
Opie's Row of Spinach Quiche
or Betty's Breakfast Grits Casserole
Courthouse Coffee Cake
Best Marble Squares

Barney orders breakfast at the Diner:
BARNEY: Let's see. I'm not too hungry this morning. I'll have, uh . . . orange juice, bowl of cereal, stack of wheats, three eggs over (make sure they ain't runny now, Olive), bacon on the crisp side, white toast buttered, hash brown potatoes, and coffee—coffee and cream.
OLIVE: Does my heart good to see a thin person eat.

Garden Club Luncheon

Tea and Coffee
Thelma Lou's Finger Sandwiches
Eleanora Poultice's A+ Fruit Salad
Helen's Honor Rolls
Diner Special Chicken and Rice Casserole
Frankly Baked Eggplant
Tears on Your Pillow Pie

Various items at the Diner:
Chicken fried steak: $1.35
Ham and lima beans: $1.30
Hamburger steak: $1.25
Pot roast plate
For the meat loaf plate, Goober uses lots of catsup.
Chicken à la king: "Real delish," says Flora.
Root beer float
Soft drinks are 5 cents.
Waffle special is 45 cents.
Hamburger
Tuna sandwich
Blueberry, apple, and peach pie
As for the meat loaf plate, Goober really likes it with fresh coffee.

Lunch with Leon

Milk
Tex Foley's Cowboy Soup
Leon's Thankless Peanut Butter and Jelly Sandwich
Apple

Mayberry's Mexican Fiesta

Miss Crump's Gold Star Gazpacho
Toss and Turn Salad
A Cappella Chicken Enchilada
Bee's Biscochitos

Blue Plate Special

Diner Rolls
Carlotta Corn Muffins with Cheese and Chilies
Checkpoint Chickie Pan Pie
Sarah's Succotash
County Clerk Creamed Carrots
or A-O.K. Fried Okra
Miss Lucy's Coconut Cake

Morelli's Pounded Steak Dinner

Floyd's Fruit and Nut Salad
Quarter Tip Rolls
Minestrone Made Right
Pounded Steak à la Morelli
Old Lady Crump's Onion Pie
Emmett's Carrots and Peas
Mom's Apple Pie in Paper Bag

Aunt Bee's Canton Palace Plate

Fun Girls Wonton
Charlie Lee's Chicken Chow Mein
Siler City Snow Peas
Paradise Rice
Goober Says Haystacks
or Loafers Lemon Lotus Ice Cream
Fortune Cookies

COL. HARVEY: Miss Bee, I have dined in the finest restaurants in New Orleans, but never have I tasted food like that.

AUNT BEE: Oh, Colonel, how can you say that? It was only just pot luck, you know.

COL. HARVEY: Toosh, my dear lady, toosh. There is pot luck and there is pot luck. Not only the ingredients—it's the magic with which it's prepared and you, my dear lady, have the magical touch. My compliments.

Southern Pork Dinner
Thelma Lou's Neighborly Popovers
Pipe Down Pork Chop Casserole
Bert and Ben's Sweet-and-Sour Green Beans
Andy's Red Hot Applesauce
Hubcaps Lesch's Lemon Chess Pie

Mayberry Meat Loaf Meal
Bee's Bingo Cherry Salad
Briscoe's Biscuits
Flora's Meat Loaf Malherbe
Emmett's Carrots and Peas
Houdini Zucchini
Al Becker's Butterscotch Pie

Howard's Caribbean Dinner
Gertrude's Rowboat Rolls
Crooner's Shrimp Creole
or Lefty's Alligator Done Right
Paradise Rice
Island Cucumbers in Vinegar
St. Benedict's Coconut Cream Pie

Barney's Steak Out
Toss and Turn Salad
Barney's Salt and Pepper Steak
Barney's Bongo Broccoli Casserole
Nip It in the Bud Spuds
Mr. Dave's Fudge "Browne" Pie

Mr. Schwamp's Vegetable Stagline
Regal Order Rolls
Ev's Vegetarian Dinner
Knot-Tying Club Noodles
or Sheriff's Rice
Barney's Banana Granola Cookies

Barney's Bachelor Supper
Mrs. Mendelbright's Hot Apple Cider
Ernest Toss Salad
Barney's Hot Plate Chili
or Five-Minute Corn and Shrimp Barney Supper
Mr. No-Bake Cookies

Aunt Bee's Southern Family Dinner
Grandma's Biscuits
Aunt Bee's Fried Chicken
Nip It in the Bud Spuds
Sly Devil Eggs
Sweet Romeena Creamed Corn
Breeney Green Beans
Opie's Turnip-Your-Nose Greens
Aunt Bee's Apple Pie

Myers Lake Catch
Gertrude's Rowboat Rolls
Ernest T.'s Bass
New Mayor Potatoes
Asa's Asparagus with Hollister Hollandaise
Bee's Gooseberry Pie

Darlings' Cabin Fever Feast
Hogette Winslow's Hogshead Cheese
Mitch's Dear Darling Venison
Cousin Toog's Bread and Butter Pickles
Warren's Rabbit Pie
Briscoe Darling's Hoot Owl Pie
Charlene's Fish Muddle
Ernest T.'s Possum and Sweet Taters
Old Man Kelsey's Barbecued Raccoon
Doug's Great White Beans
Floyd Fritters
Billie's Blueberry Dessert

Dinner at Eight Spaghetti

Cesar Romero's Lawn Salad
Italian Breadsticks with Garlic Butter or Parmesan
or Herbed Garlic Bread
Vincente Spaghetti
Goober's Secret Spaghetti Sauce
Mother Sprague's Family Spaghetti Sauce
Uncle Edward's Secret Spaghetti Sauce
Courthouse Crock Pot Spaghetti Sauce
Lemon Fluffy

Howard's Perfect Game Snacks

Assorted Bottles of Pop
Gomer's Guacamole and Tortilla Chips
Just Right Dip and Variety of Crackers
Kleptomenerac Cheese Krispies
Betty's Cheese Wafers
Howard's Scalp Level Chili
Real (Not out of a Bottle) Blondies

Howard and Andy meet on the street:

HOWARD: I see you've been doing a little shopping.

ANDY: Oh, yeah. Yeah, yeah, yeah. Wild mushrooms, canned oysters and chili sauce, pickled avocados, chocolate syrup, shrimp enchiladas.

HOWARD: That's a rather unusual assortment, isn't it?

ANDY: Does have kind of a bounce to it, doesn't it?

HOWARD: Heh-heh-heh.

ANDY: You going in, are you?

HOWARD: Oh, yeah. Mother wants (reads list): oatmeal, two quarts of whole milk, a dozen brown eggs, a container of yogurt, three dozen oranges.

ANDY: Yeah.

HOWARD: Mother likes me to get plenty of vitamin C during the flu season.

ANDY: That's very, very good thinking.

Ice Cream Social

Loafers Lemon Lotus Ice Cream
Opie's Oreo Ice Cream
Siler City Peach Cream Freeze
Cousin Bradford's Strawberry Ice Cream
Checkers Chocolate Sauce
Old-Fashioned Pound Cake
Juanita's Ginger Cookies

Bee's Missing Meal

Roger Hanover's Ham Loaf
Green Beans Chinese-Style
Newton Monroe's Pineapple Casserole
Clara's Nesselrode Pie

New Year's Day

Carolina Corn Pone
Granny's Slaw
Rafe's Red River Catfish Fry
Hollister Hoppin' John
Opie's Carrot-Top Cake

Birthday Bash

Ernest Toss Salad
Italian Breadsticks
Andrew Paul Lawson's Lasagna
Hope for More Chocolate Cake
or Andy's Chocolate-Filled Angel Food Cake
Opie's Oreo Ice Cream

Valentine's Day

Elfie's Wilted Lettuce Salad
Helen's Honor Rolls
Write-On Chicken Marsala
Ellie's Confetti Vegetables
Thelma Lou's Very Chocolate Cheesecake

St. Patrick's Day

Ernest Tea
Ernest Toss Salad
Ernest T. Bass's Chicken-Thief Stew
or Barney's Blarney Beef Stew
Blue Ridge Mountain Cornbread
Grand Grasshopper Pie

Fourth of July Backyard Barbecue

Floyd's Fiddle-Faddle
Old Sam's Better Potato Salad
Viewer's Choice of Meat for Grilling (chicken, pork, or beef)
Barbershop Barbecue Sauce
Baked Goober Beanies
Aunt Bee's Kerosene Cucumbers
Ernest T. Bass Rock Bars
Watermelon Wally

Fourth of July dessert

ANDY: That was a fine dinner, Aunt Bee. Outstandin', outstandin'.

Halloween

Toss and Turn Salad
Mayberry After Midnight Pumpkin Bread
More Power to Ya Meatballs
Knot-Tying Club Noodles
or Sheriff's Rice
Goober Says Haystacks
or Harvey's Little Big Orange Cookies

WE WISH YOU MORELLI CHRISTMAS

(Sung to the tune of "We Wish You a Merry Christmas")
Lyrics by John Hillman and William "Jingle Bill" Wardlaw

We wish you Morelli Christmas,
We wish you Morelli Christmas,
We wish you Morelli Christmas,
And red-checkered New Year.

It's out there on the highway,
It's out there on the highway,
It's out there on the highway,
Secluded and nice.

We won't take a bottle in there,
We won't take a bottle in there,
We won't take a bottle in there,
(Well, maybe just one).

Oh, bring us the Deluxe Special,
Oh, bring us the Deluxe Special,
Oh, bring us the Deluxe Special,
But let's not fill up.

We can hold it to $1.85,
We can hold it to $1.85,
We can hold it to $1.85,
If we don't have the shrimp.

The minestrone is delicious,
The minestrone is delicious,
The minestrone is delicious,
When it's made just right.

The steaks are well pounded,
The steaks are well pounded,
The steaks are well pounded,
You can see with your own eyes.

We'll send compliments to the chef,
We'll send compliments to the chef,
We'll send compliments to the chef,
And he'll sort of just wave.

We'll tip the gypsy violinist,
We'll tip the gypsy violinist,
We'll tip the gypsy violinist,
But he'll be moody though.

We wish you Morelli Christmas,
We wish you Morelli Christmas,
We wish you Morelli Christmas,
Now let's have that bottle.*
*Just in case Otis joins us

Holiday Dinner

Great-Grandmother Minnie's Rolls
Aunt Bee's Turkey Dinner with Stuffing
Robert E. Lee Natural Bridge Sweet Tater Pone
Goober Peas
or Breeney Green Beans
Sweet Romeena Creamed Corn
Cranberry Sauce Crump
Praline Pumpkin Pie Juanita
Aunt Bee's Blue Ribbon Rhubarb Pie
Mt. Pilot Pecan Pie
Oranges and Grapefruit

Holiday Party

Wally's Wassail
Emmett's Cuckoo Clock Cocoa Mix
Tampico Tortilla Roll-Ups
Just Right Dip
Aw Gee, Paw Cheese Ball
Minuteman Quiches
Cousin Leda's Banana Chutney
Ben Weaver's Christmas Cut-Out Cookies
Ernest T. Bass's Nutty Fruit Cake
Johnny Paul Jason's Pralines
Pearson's Peppermints

AUNT BEE: I love to cook.

Mayberry Premiere
(Cast and Crew Specialties)

Thelma Lou's Neighborly Popovers
Howard's Scalp Level Chili
Orange Chicken Helen
Ellie's Confetti Vegetables
Dean Darling's Pineapple-Banana Nut Snack Cake
Opie and Leon's Favorite Buttermilk Pie

High noon at the courthouse:

BARNEY: Well, where's Aunt Bee with lunch? She's usually here and gone by now.

ANDY: She's a little late.

BARNEY: Well, I'm hungry, Ange.

ANDY: She'll be along in a few minutes. Relax.

BARNEY: Well, I happen to have this low-sugar blood content, and if I don't get my lunch by noon then I get a headache and I'm no good to anybody.

ANDY: A few minutes one way or the other shouldn't make any difference.

BARNEY: Well, it does to me. I've got a clock in my stomach.

ANDY: You must have.

BARNEY: I go by that clock, too. Tick, tick. I know it's time for lunch. Tick, tick. I know it's time for dinner. My mother was the same way.

ANDY: I remember that about your mother.

BARNEY: She had a clock in her stomach.

ANDY: Hey, Barn? These clocks you and your mother had in your stomachs? Did the tickin' keep your father awake at night?

BARNEY: You wanna get facetious? You wanna get facetious about the whole thing? Is that what you want to do—get facetious?

ANDY: No.

BARNEY: Well, just don't get facetious. That happens to be a very common thing: clock in the stomach.

ANDY: I know, I know, I know. Aunt Bee had an elephant she kept on the mantelpiece, and it had a clock in its stomach. Now, don't get mad. I was just kidding.

BARNEY: I don't mind you kiddin' me about my stomach, but don't kid about my mother's stomach.

Andy Taylor

Andy is Mayberry's "sheriff without a gun." He oversees justice not so much by the book, but by the heart. With his commonsense approach to life, fatherhood, and friendship, Andy helps make Mayberry a wonderful place to live.

Although Andy has many talents, cooking is not one of them. Fortunately, he and son Opie are nourished by Aunt Bee—in more ways than one. They particularly appreciate her homemade meals. Andy has a special taste for leg of lamb, fried chicken, and gooseberry and pumpkin pies.

All in all, no one adds more flavor to Mayberry than Andy.

Appetizers

A Blessing

After you've prepared your meal from some of the delicious recipes in *Aunt Bee's Mayberry Cookbook*, how about starting your meal with Robert Louis Stevenson's blessing:

> Thank you for the world so sweet,
> Thank you for the food we eat,
> Thank you for the birds that sing,
> Thank you, Lord, for everything.

Submitted by Helen C. Myers—Sacramento, California

Cheesy F.B.I. Man Safe Crackers

Picture perfect.

$1/2$ cup butter
2 tablespoons tomato juice
2 cups grated cheddar cheese
1 cup sifted all-purpose flour

$3/4$ cup chopped pecans
$1/4$ teaspoon red pepper
$1/2$ teaspoon salt

In a large bowl cream together the butter and tomato juice. Add the remaining ingredients. Divide the mixture in half and roll into 2 rolls about 12 inches long. Chill overnight.

Cut the rolls into slices about $1/4$-inch thick and arrange on an ungreased cookie sheet. Bake in a 350° oven for 10 to 12 minutes.

Serves 6 to 8.

Cordelia Kelly—Greensboro, North Carolina

In the courthouse, Andy and Barney discuss being pursued by women:

BARNEY: You know, a few years back a similar thing happened to me.

ANDY: Yeah?

BARNEY: Maybe I never told you about it. The girl's name was Halcyon Loretta Winslow.

ANDY: Pretty name.

BARNEY: Ugliest girl you ever saw in your life. What happened was her father got it in his head that I should marry Halcyon. You know, he saw my picture in the paper. You remember when I won that church raffle—four free haircuts?

ANDY: Oh, yeah. Picture's all over the front page.

BARNEY: Well, you know how that affects people. They go crazy. Right away, he saw civil servant—security. Right? Then he saw unmarried, and at the time I was only three-o.

ANDY: Thirty.

BARNEY: Right. He saw in me an untapped source of lifetime happiness for his ugly daughter. So, needless to say they got my phone number from the barber and the rest is history.

ANDY: I don't believe I ever heard of it.

BARNEY: You didn't? Well, I tell you, it's like a tale out of two cities. First, I only saw the old man for about a week. He made me a tempting offer: third interest in a prune-pitting operation.

ANDY: There's a lot of money in that.

BARNEY: Well, you got to like it. Full use of the company car, an interest in the family home, and a beautiful hillside plot in the Mt. Pilot cemetery.

ANDY: That burial plot alone is worth a fortune.

BARNEY: You know me. When opportunity knocks, ol' Barn's got to at least take a peek and see if there's anybody on the stoop. Anyway, the old man made a date for all of us to meet down at Klein's Coffeehouse for American cheese and garni.

ANDY: Yeah, finally met her, huh?

BARNEY: Oh, boy.

ANDY: Not too pretty?

BARNEY: Beasto maristo. I'll tell you that cheese sandwich stuck right there (points at Adam's apple) for about three days.

ANDY: How'd you finally get off the hook?

BARNEY: Well, first of all, paid for my own cheese sandwich.

ANDY: Wipe out any obligations.

BARNEY: Right. Then I took the old man to one side, and I told him straight out N-O, a flat no dice. . . . But he kept after me, letters, phone calls, driving that company car by all shiny and new. But I held my ground. Pretty soon he got the idea, and that was the end of it.

ANDY: Whatever happened to Halcyon?

BARNEY: Well, you know she went east to one of them schools where they trim you down, clear your skin, make you walk around with a book on your head.

ANDY: Don't tell me—she turned out to be beautiful?

BARNEY: No. She's still ugly, single, and pittin' prunes.

Betty's Cheese Wafers

1/2 cup butter
2 cups shredded sharp cheddar cheese
1 teaspoon Worcestershire sauce

Dash Tabasco
1 cup sifted all-purpose flour

In a food processor or electric mixer, combine all of the ingredients. Roll into logs, cover, and refrigerate until firm.

Grease a cookie sheet. Slice into wafers and place on the cookie sheet. Bake in a 350° oven for 12 minutes.

Serves 6.

Harvey Bullock—writer

Kleptomenerac Cheese Krispies

They'll steal your taste buds.

1 12-ounce package sharp cheddar cheese
1 cup margarine
2 cups all-purpose flour

1 cup self-rising flour
2 cups Rice Krispies

In a large saucepan over low heat melt the cheese and margarine together. Remove from the heat and add the flour. Stir in the Rice Krispies and mix thoroughly. Roll into small balls and place on a cookie sheet. Bake in a 325° oven for 15 minutes.

Serves 6.

Bobbie Carson—Nashville, Tennessee

Thelma Lou's Finger Sandwiches

1/2 cup grated cheddar cheese
1/2 cup butter, melted
2 eggs, beaten
1/2 teaspoon onion salt

1/2 teaspoon garlic salt
Paprika
Bread slices with crusts removed

With a mixer combine the cheese, butter, eggs, onion salt, and garlic salt. Cut each slice of bread into 4 square pieces. Place a spoonful of the cheese mixture on half of the bread squares, and top with the remaining bread squares. Top with another spoonful of the cheese mixture. Sprinkle with paprika and arrange on a cookie sheet. Bake in a 400° oven for 10 minutes.

Serves 6 to 8.

Tina Muncy—Clarksville, Arkansas

Goober and girlfriend Lydia drop by for a visit:
> **HELEN:** Lydia, would you care for a pretzel?
> **LYDIA:** No, thank you. They lay on my chest.
> **HELEN:** I'm sorry. Goober?
> **GOOBER:** Yo!
> **BARNEY:** (To Andy) Not much lays on his chest.

Tampico Tortilla Roll-Ups

You'll develop a "compelsion" for these taste bud tempters.

2 8-ounce packages cream cheese
1 8-ounce carton sour cream
2 to 3 green onions, finely chopped
Juice of 1/2 lime

2 to 3 fresh jalapeño peppers, chopped
12 fresh flour tortillas
Salsa

In a bowl combine the cream cheese, sour cream, onions, lime juice, and jalapeño peppers. Blend well. Spread the filling on the tortillas. Roll up the tortillas and cut into 1-inch rolls. Cover with a wet towel and chill until ready to serve.

Serve with salsa.

Serves 6.

Leslie Hay—Nashville, Tennessee

Barney's Cock-a-Doodle-Doo Canapé

No phony business here. It's for real.

Cream cheese
Anchovy paste
Toasted bread rounds
Ham slices (optional)
Tomato slices

Hard-boiled egg slices
1 dill pickle, finely chopped
1 small onion, finely chopped
1 pint mayonnaise
1 teaspoon chopped parsley

Combine cream cheese and a small amount of anchovy paste. Spread toasted rounds of bread with the cream cheese mixture. Place a slice of ham, tomato, and egg over each.

Combine the remaining ingredients and place a small amount of the tartar sauce mixture over each canapé. Arrange on a serving tray and serve at once.

Mrs. Edward Kuhn—Charlotte, North Carolina

Mrs. Mendelbright's Stuffed Mushrooms

From her best cellar.

80 mushrooms
1/2 cup butter, melted
3/4 cup Parmesan cheese

1/2 cup mushroom stems, chopped
1/2 teaspoon garlic salt
1 8-ounce package cream cheese, softened

Line baking sheets with foil. Wash and remove the stems from the mushrooms. Chop and reserve 1/2 cup of the stems. Brush the caps with the butter and place on the trays. In a medium bowl combine the Parmesan, mushroom stems, garlic salt, and cream cheese, blending well. Fill the caps with the mixture. Bake in a 350° oven for 15 minutes.

These may be frozen. Bake an additional 5 minutes.

Makes 80 stuffed mushrooms.

Aw Gee, Paw Cheese Ball

2 8-ounce packages cream cheese
1 8-ounce can pineapple tidbits
2 tablespoons chopped onion

1/4 cup chopped green pepper
2 cups chopped pecans
1/4 teaspoon salt

With a fork cream the cream cheese. Add the remaining ingredients, reserving 1 cup of pecans. Mix well by hand. Let the mixture harden in the refrigerator for 45 minutes. Remove and shape into a ball. Roll in the reserved pecans.

Makes 1 really big cheese ball or 1 sort of big one and 1 little one.

Shelia Cox—Nashville, Tennessee

Rugged farmer Jeff Pruitt is introduced to the delicate ways of city living:

JEFF PRUITT: Honey pie, somebody got in your food and tore it into little teeny pieces.
THELMA LOU: Oh, silly boy. They're finger sandwiches. Wel-ll . . .
JEFF: Kinda good. Whets my appetite for supper.
THELMA LOU: Why, Jeff, this is supper.
JEFF: You're joking!
THELMA LOU: Why, no.
JEFF: Can you honestly call this a meal?
THELMA LOU: I believe in keeping trim.
JEFF: Trim! Why, there ain't enough meal there to—get skinny on!

Andy and rich girlfriend Peggy dine at a fancy Raleigh restaurant:
ANDY: What's that?
PEGGY: Escargots, snails! You've had some, haven't you?
ANDY: No, I've stepped on quite a few of 'em in my time. But I never have eaten one of 'em. . . . I believe I'll just let the snails go by.

Just Right Dip

Perfect when the chips are down.

1 14 1/2-ounce can asparagus spears, drained
1/2 cup sour cream

1/4 teaspoon hot sauce
1 teaspoon dried dill weed
1 teaspoon seasoned salt

In a blender combine all of the ingredients, and whip until smooth. Adjust the seasonings to taste. Serve with corn chips.

Serves 6 to 8.

Miracle Salve Dip

Tested and approved by Dr. Pendyke.

9 slices bacon
3 small tomatoes, quartered
1 8-ounce package cream cheese, softened and cubed
3 teaspoons prepared mustard

1/4 teaspoon Tabasco sauce
1 1/2 cups almonds
3 tablespoons chopped green onions
Crackers

In a large skillet fry the bacon. Drain on paper towels, crumble, and set aside. In a blender or food processor blend the tomatoes, cream cheese, mustard, and Tabasco sauce. Add the almonds, onions, and bacon, and blend until the almonds are chopped. Refrigerate for 2 hours or up to 2 days. Serve with crackers.

Serves 10 to 12.

OPIE: I think I'll split over there and get some of those cool-looking potato chips.

Miracle Salve salesmen

No Heartaches Artichoke Dip

1 cup mayonnaise
1 cup Parmesan cheese

1 6-ounce can artichoke hearts

In an ovenproof bowl combine the mayonnaise and Parmesan cheese. Drain the artichokes and add to the mixture. Bake in a 350° oven for 20 to 30 minutes.

    Serves 6.

Laina Bush—McLean, Virginia

Gomer's Guacamole and Tortilla Chips

Shazam!

2 cups all-purpose flour
1 teaspoon salt
1 teaspoon baking powder
1 tablespoon lard or shortening
1/2 to 3/4 cup warm water (110°)
Oil
Salt to taste

2 medium avocados, seeded, peeled, and
   cut up
1/2 small onion, cut up
2 tablespoons lemon juice
1 clove garlic, minced
1/2 teaspoon salt
1/4 teaspoon pepper

In a mixing bowl stir together the flour, salt, and baking powder. Cut in the lard until the mixture resembles cornmeal. Add 1/2 cup of water and stir until the dough can be gathered into a ball. If needed, add more water, 1 tablespoon at a time. Let the dough rest for 15 minutes. Divide the dough into 12 portions and shape into balls. Turn onto a lightly floured board and roll each ball into a 7-inch round. Trim uneven edges to make round tortillas. Stack the rounds and cut the stack into 6 wedges.

In a deep skillet heat 1/2 inch of oil. Fry the wedges a few at a time for about 45 seconds, or until they are crisp and lightly browned. Drain well on paper toweling. Sprinkle the chips lightly with salt.

In a blender container combine the remaining ingredients. Cover and blend until well combined. Serve with Tortilla Chips.

Serves 6 to 8.

Hello Country Bumpkin Pumpkin Seeds

A pit hit.

2 cups pumpkin seeds
1 1/2 tablespoons oil
Salt

Wash and wipe the seeds. Coat with the oil, and spread on a baking sheet. Sprinkle with salt. Bake in a 350° oven for 20 to 30 minutes, or in a 150° oven for 2 to 4 hours. They pop when done, but need to be watched.

Store in an airtight jar.

Makes 2 cups.

Jennifer Trumbull—Nashville, Tennessee

Dinner at Morelli's

Old Man Kelsey's Deer Jerky

1 1/2 to 2 pounds lean boneless deer meat,
   partially frozen
1/4 cup soy sauce
1 tablespoon Worcestershire sauce
1/4 teaspoon ground pepper

1/4 teaspoon garlic powder
1/4 teaspoon onion powder
1/4 teaspoon hickory smoked salt
1/4 cup firmly packed brown sugar
1 small bottle liquid smoke

Trim all fat from the meat. Slice the meat as thinly as possible. In a bowl combine the remaining ingredients. Stir until dissolved. Add the meat and mix well. Cover and refrigerate overnight.

Shake the excess liquid from the meat and arrange in a shallow pan or cookie sheet. Dry the meat in a 150° to 200° oven until dry and brown, a minimum of 8 hours. Cool, remove from the pan, and store in a glass jar.

Note: If spicy hot jerky is desired, you may sprinkle coarsely ground black pepper over the meat just before placing it in the oven.

Timothy Thompson—Manvel, Texas

Dipper deputy

Beverages

Ernest Tea

T-licious!

7 tea bags
12 sprigs mint
Rind of 3 lemons
8 cups boiling water

Juice of 7 lemons
2 cups sugar
8 cups cold water

Steep the tea, mint, and lemon rind in the boiling water for 12 minutes. Remove the tea, mint, and lemon rind from the water. Add the lemon juice and sugar, and strain. Add the cold water.
  Makes 1 gallon.

Russian Summit Tea

Everyone agrees it's tops.

1 12-ounce can frozen orange juice
  concentrate
2 6-ounce cans frozen limeade concentrate
1 6-ounce can frozen lemonade concentrate
1 1/2 cups water
Juice of 8 lemons

Juice of 2 oranges
12 cups prepared tea
3 cups pineapple-grapefruit juice (1/2 large
  can) or 2 cups pineapple juice and 1 cup
  grapefruit juice
Sugar to taste, approx. 2/3 cup

In a pitcher or large container combine all of the ingredients. Stir until well blended and sweeten to taste.
  Serves 12.

Julia Cuthbertson—Charlotte, North Carolina

AUNT BEE: Oh, dear, if I knew there was going to be a summit meeting in my kitchen,
I would have washed the floor.

Ready for Mrs. Wiley

Mayberry socialite Mrs. Wiley describes her encounter with a "creature" named Ernest T. Bass.

MRS. WILEY: And then he burst into the house uninvited and started behaving in the most peculiar manner.

ANDY: Like what, Mrs. Wiley?

MRS. WILEY: Oh, uh, well, he stuck his hand in the punch bowl, and he ate every bit of the watermelon rind. And if that wasn't enough, he soaked the paper napkins in the punch, and then he threw them at the ceiling.

ANDY: Well, didn't anybody try to stop him?

MRS. WILEY: Mr. Schwamp—tried to pinch him, but he just giggled and jumped away.

Opie's Lemonade

Best served fresh and frosty.

6 lemons
1 1/2 cups sugar

2 1/2 quarts water

Slice the lemons into thin rings. Place in a porcelain or enamel container. Add the sugar and pound with a wooden mallet to extract the juice. Let the mixture stand for 20 minutes.
     Add the cold water and ice cubes as desired. Stir until well blended.
     Makes 3 quarts.

Janie Love—Hermitage, Tennessee

Wally's Wassail

6 cups apple cider or juice
1 stick cinnamon
1/4 teaspoon nutmeg
1/4 cup honey

3 tablespoons lemon juice
1 teaspoon lemon rind
1 20-ounce can unsweetened pineapple
  juice

In a large pan heat the cider and cinnamon stick. Bring to a boil. Reduce the heat, cover, and simmer for 5 minutes. Add the remaining ingredients and simmer uncovered for 5 minutes. Keep over low heat or reheat in small batches as guests arrive.
     Makes 20 cups.

Margaret Hooper—Houston, Texas

Mrs. Mendelbright's Hot Apple Cider

Perfect for front-porch sipping while counting the cars that go by.

1/3 cup firmly packed brown sugar
Dash salt
2 quarts apple juice

1 teaspoon whole cloves
1 3-inch stick cinnamon

In a large saucepan combine all of the ingredients. Mix well and simmer for a few minutes.
     Makes 2 quarts.

Mrs. Frank Brower—Asheboro, North Carolina

AUNT BEE: Opie, you haven't finished your milk. We can't put it back in the cow, you know.

Otis Campbell

Mayberry's most famous consumer of spirits is nobody's fool. He knows how to make sure he gets a good breakfast after a night on the town. He just heads for the courthouse, turns himself in for the night, and then wakes up to the smell of one of Aunt Bee's good breakfasts.

On the other hand, he did have a rude awakening the time when the jail was too full and he had to be incarcerated at the Taylor house with Aunt Bee as the warden. Although it was a sobering experience, it didn't rock Otis for long. He was soon on to his merry ways again.

Emmett's Cuckoo Clock Cocoa Mix

Great anytime.

2 cups coffee creamer

1 cup sugar

$^3/_4$ cup cocoa

$^1/_2$ cup nonfat powdered milk

In a glass jar or container with an airtight lid, combine all of the ingredients and mix well. Cover and store until needed.

Add 2 tablespoons of mix to 1 cup of water for a quick cup of hot cocoa. *Makes about 34 servings.*

Mary Jane Hamilton—Houston, Texas

One-Punch Opie Pineapple Punch

A knockout.

1 46-ounce can pineapple juice, chilled

3 cups apricot nectar

1 quart club soda

1 quart pineapple sherbet

In a large punch bowl combine the pineapple juice and apricot nectar. Just before serving, add the club soda and sherbet.

Makes 25 to 30 servings.

Mary Ann McNeese—Nashville, Tennessee

BOTTLES OF POP QUIZ

1. According to Floyd, where can you get the best bottles of pop in Mayberry?
   Answer: Wally's Filling Station
2. Who spiked the water crock in the Mayberry courthouse?
   Answer: Otis
3. Where in Mayberry can you expect to get a lemon phosphate?
   Answer: The drugstore
4. What is the beverage of choice at the Regal Order of the Golden Door to Good Fellowship?
   Answer: Root beer
5. What does Otis say his hobby is?
   Answer: Drinking

RECIPE: Andy's Punch Supreme: Orange sherbet, tomato juice, root beer, and molasses.

Goober's Radiator Flush Punch

The color is that of slightly rusty radiator fluid.

2 cups prepared tea
Juice of 2 oranges
1 12-ounce can orange soda

Juice of 1 lemon
1 cup ginger ale
Orange and lemon slices

In a pitcher combine all of the ingredients. Serve over ice.
   This is best when served with comic books.
   Makes 5 cups.

Bill Flynn—High Point, North Carolina

Leonard Blush Fruit Slush

Out of sight!

4 cups warm water
3 cups sugar
4 bananas, mashed
1 6-ounce can frozen orange juice
   concentrate

1 6-ounce can frozen lemonade concentrate
1 cup orange instant breakfast drink
   (optional)
1 46-ounce can pineapple juice
7-Up or ginger ale

In a large container combine the warm water and sugar, stirring until dissolved. Add the mashed bananas and the juices. Freeze the mixture.
   Remove the mixture from the freezer 30 minutes before serving. Scoop into glasses and pour 7-Up or ginger ale over the frozen mixture.
   Makes about 26 servings.

Juanita Sullivan—Albuquerque, New Mexico

RECIPE: Warren's hangover cure, an old remedy: Sassafrass root, sorghum molasses, and a raw egg and hot sauce. Mix it all up.

OTIS: I came to fill my vase.

Golleee Gelatin Punch

By golleee, it's good!

1 6-ounce box strawberry gelatin
2 cups boiling water
2 cups cold water

1 cup sugar
1 pint cranberry juice
1 2-liter bottle ginger ale

Dissolve the gelatin in the boiling water. Add the sugar and stir until the sugar dissolves, but do not boil. Add the cold water and let the mixture cool, but not congeal. Pour into a punch bowl and add the cranberry juice. Add the ginger ale just before serving.

Serves 12.

Ramona Richards—Nashville, Tennessee

Once a man moves to Raleigh, he becomes worldly:
BARNEY: I'd like to make a reservation. Table for two about quarter past one. . . . Yeah. . . . B. Fife. . . . That's right. Oh, and listen—put a bottle of your best red wine on ice for me, will you? . . . Room temperature? Oh, well, that's a matter of taste.

Selecting a beverage can be a hard choice.

Ellie Walker

For many, Ellie is just what the doctor ordered for Mayberry. She is easily Mayberry's most unforgettable pharmacist. Her prescription for Mayberry is savvy, charm, beauty, and, as Andy is quick to note, "an awful handsome brain."

While in Mayberry, Ellie dispenses with several weary traditions. For example, Miss Walker is the first woman to run for a seat on the town council (she also wins). As a leading lady in Mayberry, Ellie frequently matches wits with Andy. But even Andy's no match for one of her soda fountain concoctions made with castor oil.

Soups

Miss Crump's Gold Star Gazpacho

2 large ripe tomatoes
1 large sweet green pepper
1 clove garlic
Salt to taste
1/2 cup chopped mixed herbs (chives,
    parsley, basil, chervil, tarragon)
1/2 cup olive oil

3 tablespoons lemon or lime juice
3 cups chilled water
1 sweet Spanish onion, peeled and diced
1 cup peeled, seeded, and diced cucumber
1 1/2 teaspoons salt or to taste
1/2 teaspoon paprika

Peel and seed the tomatoes. Seed and remove the membrane from the pepper. Cube, chop, or dice the tomatoes, pepper, and garlic. In a large bowl combine the chopped tomatoes, pepper, and garlic, and add salt. Add the herbs. Gradually stir in the oil, lemon juice, and water. Add the remaining ingredients. Chill for at least 4 hours. Cold and crunchy!

Aneta Corsaut—cast member

Aunt Bee's Lentil Soup

Hard to pass up.

1 pound smoked sausage (large link), sliced
1 pound lentils
1/2 cup chopped onion
1/2 cup sliced celery
1/2 cup sliced carrots
1/8 teaspoon garlic salt

2 1/2 teaspoons salt
1 1/2 teaspoons oregano
1 6-ounce can tomato paste
8 cups water
1 20-ounce can tomatoes

In a large stock pot combine all of the ingredients except the tomatoes. Cook for 1 hour and 30 minutes. Add the tomatoes and simmer for 30 minutes.
    Serves 12.

Tina Muncy—Clarksville, Arkansas

Tex Foley's Cowboy Soup

A runaway success.

1 pound ground beef
1/2 cup chopped onion
1 16-ounce can mixed vegetables
1 10-ounce can Rotel tomatoes

1 13-ounce can Spanish rice
1 14 1/2-ounce can stewed tomatoes
1 17-ounce can cream-style corn

In a large stock pot brown the ground beef and onion. Add the remaining ingredients, cover, and simmer for about 1 hour.

Serves 6.

Patsy Curtis—Charlotte, Tennessee

Otis Campbell's Homemade Vegetable Soup

M-mm, m-mm great!

6 cups chicken broth
1 15-ounce can tomato sauce
4 medium potatoes, diced
2 carrots, chopped
1/2 onion, chopped
1/4 cup chopped celery tops and pieces
1/4 cup chopped green pepper

1 handful uncooked rice
1 teaspoon basil
1/2 teaspoon parsley
1/2 teaspoon dill
1/2 teaspoon pepper
1 teaspoon Worcestershire sauce
1 1/2 teaspoons salt

Usually I boil skinned chicken pieces for about 2 hours to obtain the broth. I add the above listed items and other leftover vegetables like green beans and corn if they are available. Bring the broth to a boil and then simmer for about 1 hour.

The soup lasts well in the refrigerator for up to a week and can be frozen.

Serves 6 to 8.

Edna Skinner—Montreal, Quebec

Summit summary:
MR. CLIFFORD: My congratulations to whoever steered us here—to a quiet, informal meeting in a homey kitchen with a charming, charming hostess.

Extry Good Potato Soup

3 potatoes, peeled
1 quart milk
3 slices onion
3 tablespoons butter
2 tablespoons all-purpose flour

1 1/2 teaspoons salt
1/4 teaspoon celery salt
1/8 teaspoon pepper
Few grains cayenne pepper
1 teaspoon chopped parsley

Cook the potatoes in salted water. When soft, rub through a strainer. There should be 2 1/2 cups. Scald the milk with onion, remove the onion, and slowly whisk the milk into the potatoes. Melt half of the butter and add the flour, salt, celery salt, pepper, and cayenne. Stir until well mixed, then stir into the hot soup. Boil for 1 minute, strain, and add the remaining butter. Sprinkle with parsley.

Serves 4 to 6.

Janie Love—Hermitage, Tennessee

Jud's Broccoli Cheese Soup

Soup for all ages.

1 cup water
1 chicken bouillon cube
1 10-ounce package frozen chopped
 broccoli
1 medium carrot, grated
2 tablespoons butter
3 tablespoons all-purpose flour

2 cups milk
1 pound processed American cheese,
 cubed
1 10 1/2-ounce can cream of chicken soup
1 tablespoon minced onion flakes
1 tablespoon Worcestershire sauce
Salt and pepper to taste

In a saucepan bring the water and bouillon cube to a boil. Add the broccoli and carrot. Cook according to the broccoli package directions, and remove from the heat. Do not drain. In a separate saucepan melt the butter and slowly stir in the flour. Continue stirring while gradually adding the milk. Stir in the cheese, soup, onion, Worcestershire sauce, salt, and pepper. Add the broccoli mixture to the white sauce mixture and cook over medium to low heat until the soup is the desired thickness.

Serves 6 to 8.

Minestrone Made Right

1 pound fresh spinach
1/2 cup fine bread crumbs (made from toast)
1 1/2 pounds lean ground beef
1 egg
Salt and pepper to taste
3 tablespoons oil
1 16-ounce can tomatoes, broken up with
   a spoon
2 cups cooked kidney beans (or 1 16-ounce
   can)

1 large onion, finely chopped
1 1/2 cups chopped celery
1 cup sliced carrots
1/2 teaspoon oregano
1/2 teaspoon basil
1 cup uncooked elbow macaroni
2 quarts beef broth
Parmesan cheese

Wash the spinach and remove the stems. Dry and finely chop the spinach. In a bowl combine the spinach, toast crumbs, beef, egg, salt, and pepper. Shape into meatballs about 1 inch in diameter. In a large kettle or Dutch oven, heat the oil. Add as many of the meatballs as will fit and brown thoroughly on all sides. Remove with a slotted spoon and repeat until all of the balls are browned. Keep the meatballs warm in a separate dish. Add the onion to the kettle and cook until translucent. Add the tomatoes, beans, oregano, basil, and beef broth. Simmer covered for 15 minutes. Add the carrots and celery, and simmer for about 10 minutes more. Stir in the macaroni, and simmer until it is done, about 10 minutes or so. Spoon into serving bowls and sprinkle with Parmesan.
   Serves 6.

Gene Wyatt—Nashville, Tennessee

Vasilievich Borscht

No matter how you say it, it's a success.

1 pound cooked beets
3 14-ounce cans beef broth
1/3 cup vinegar
1 teaspoon salt

1 small carrot, finely chopped
1 teaspoon dill weed
1 1/2 cups sour cream

In a large kettle combine all of the ingredients except the sour cream. Bring to a boil, reduce the heat, and simmer for 30 minutes. After it cools a bit, whirl in a blender until smooth (it will take several batches). Chill in the refrigerator for several hours, or preferably overnight.
   Spoon into serving bowls and top with a healthy dollop of sour cream. Stir slightly.

Note: You may use canned beets, but if the beets are cooked from scratch, be sure not to peel them until after they are done. This preserves the color.

Serves 6.

Gene Wyatt—Nashville, Tennessee

Ernest T. Bass's Chicken-Thief Stew

Ernest T. doesn't chew his cabbage twice, but he always comes back for more of this.

All-purpose flour
1 4-pound chicken, cut in pieces
1/2 cup oil
1/2 cup chopped onion
3 cups canned tomatoes
1 cup water

1 1/2 tablespoons salt
1 tablespoon Worcestershire sauce
1/4 teaspoon cayenne pepper
2 teaspoons sugar
3 cups whole kernel corn
3 cups lima beans

Flour the chicken. In a large stock pot brown the chicken in the oil. Add the onions and cook until the onions are clear, stirring occasionally. Add the tomatoes, water, and seasonings. Cover and simmer until the chicken is almost tender. Take the chicken out of the stew and remove the bones and skin. Leave the chicken meat in fairly large pieces. Return the chicken to the stew and add the corn and lima beans. Continue cooking until the vegetables are tender. Serve hot.

Variation: If preferred, 2 pounds of boneless cubed veal or beef may be substituted, but stolen chicken is cheaper.

Serves 8.

Alice and Jim Schwenke—Houston, Texas

ERNEST T.: (Practicing his talking with Andy) How . . . do . . . you . . . do . . . Mrs. Wi-ley?

ANDY: Now that's coming along pretty good. Now try talking through your mouth more. You're twangin'. You seem to be talking through your nose.

ERNEST T.: Uh, well, I do that so's I can talk whilst I eat.

ANDY: Let's just keep working on it.

Barney's Blarney Beef Stew

Charming and so on.

1 1/2 pounds chuck roast, cut into bite-size chunks
1 cup celery, cut into chunks
4 carrots, chunked
2 or 3 medium potatoes, cut into chunks
1 onion, sliced
1/2 cup fresh bread crumbs

1 20-ounce can tomatoes
1 tablespoon salt
2 tablespoons sugar
3 tablespoons minute tapioca
3 generous splashes Worcestershire sauce
Dash oregano (optional)

In a baking dish with a tight-fitting lid combine all of the ingredients. Do not brown the meat. Cover. Bake in a 250° oven for 5 to 6 hours. Don't hurry the stew, as the long cooking time and slow oven are the key to its success.

Serves 4 to 6.

Lorraine Whitler—Nashville, Tennessee

Lucky Lindy's Lamb and Lima Bean Stew

Passes with flying colors.

2 tablespoons oil
3 pounds boneless lamb stew meat
1 onion, chopped
1 carrot, chopped
1 rib celery, chopped
4 cloves garlic, minced
1 tablespoon dried rosemary leaves

1/2 cup white wine
2 cups chicken stock
1 16-ounce can plum tomatoes
1 teaspoon salt
1 teaspoon pepper
2 10-ounce packages frozen lima beans

In a Dutch oven heat the oil and brown the lamb on all sides. Remove the lamb and drain all but 1 tablespoon of the fat. Add the onion, carrot, and celery. Cover and cook over medium-low heat until the vegetables soften, about 5 minutes. Add the garlic and rosemary, and cook for 1 minute. Add the wine and chicken stock, and simmer for 2 minutes, scraping up brown bits from the bottom of the pot. Add the lamb, any accumulated juices, the tomatoes, salt, and pepper, and simmer partially covered until the lamb is tender, about 1 hour and 30 minutes. Add the lima beans to the pot and cook until tender, 10 to 15 minutes. Skim the fat, and adjust the seasonings to taste.

Serves 8.

Thelma Lou's Oyster Stew

1 1-pint jar oysters
Small white celery stalks with leaves from
   the center of the stalk, chopped
$1/4$ cup butter or margarine
$3/4$ teaspoon salt
$1/8$ teaspoon pepper

$1/4$ teaspoon paprika
1 quart milk
Paprika
Butter
Oyster crackers

In a 2-quart saucepan heat the butter over low heat until it begins to bubble. Add the chopped celery, saving some of the green leaves. Stir and cook for a few minutes. Add the oysters and cook for 3 to 4 minutes, or until the edges of the oysters curl. Remove from the heat and add the milk, salt, pepper, and paprika. Return to the heat, and cook until almost boiling, about 10 minutes. During the last few minutes, add the reserved celery leaves. Serve in hot bowls with a lump of butter and a dash of paprika in each bowl. Serve the crackers on the side.
   Serves 6.

Betty Lynn—cast member

Barney's Hot Plate Chili

A boardinghouse favorite.

3 buds garlic
1 tablespoon oil (not olive oil)
3 pounds ground beef
2 16-ounce cans tomatoes
2 16-ounce cans red beans (pinto, kidney,
   etc.)

1 generous tablespoon cumin seed
   (or 2 teaspoons ground cumin)
1 teaspoon oregano (the secret ingredient)
3 tablespoons chili powder, at least
1 tablespoon vinegar
Salt to taste

In a heavy pan with a tight lid sauté the garlic buds in the oil. Remove the garlic and add the ground beef. Cook slowly until the red is gone from the meat and it has a slight crust. Add the tomatoes and red beans and stir together lightly. Add seasonings to taste. Simmer for 3 hours, stirring occasionally. Serve hot with crackers, corn chips, or corn pone.
   Chili is better after it has cooled and the fat has been removed.
   Serves 6 to 8.

Tonya Hamel—Greensboro, North Carolina

ERNEST T.: No coffee tea or punch thank you.

25

Chili reception by Mrs. Mendelbright

Barney's Fort Lauderdale Chili

A not-too-well-kept secret from Mrs. Mendelbright.

6 tablespoons oil
3 cups chopped onion
6 cloves garlic
2 green peppers, thickly sliced
4 1/2 pounds ground beef
1 1/2 cups boiling water
3 pounds tomatoes
3 6-ounce cans tomato paste
24 ounces tomato sauce
4 1/2 tablespoons chili powder

3 teaspoons all-purpose flour
6 tablespoons water
1 1/2 teaspoons salt
1 1/2 teaspoons pepper
3 tablespoons cumin
Worcestershire sauce to taste
Bay leaves to taste
Tabasco to taste
Red pepper to taste
6 16-ounce cans kidney beans, undrained

In a large kettle heat the oil. Sauté the onions, garlic, and green pepper until tender. Add the ground beef and cook until browned, breaking up the chunks with a fork. Add the remaining ingredients except the kidney beans, and cover. Simmer for 1 hour. Add the kidney beans and simmer for 30 minutes. Remove the green pepper rings before serving. Add beef stock if too thick.
Serves 24.

Mrs. James E. Dunn Jr.—Greensboro, North Carolina

Señor Hal's Prize Chili

A nacho 'bove the rest.

2 strips bacon, fried
2 pounds boneless stew meat, cut into
   1/2-inch cubes
2 medium onions, chopped
2 medium fresh jalapeño peppers, diced
1 14 1/2-ounce can stewed tomatoes
1 6-ounce can tomato paste

1 ounce Mexene chili powder
1 ounce Louisiana Hot Sauce
1 teaspoon cumin
Salt to taste
1 pound ground beef
2 16-ounce cans pinto beans

In a large chili pot fry the bacon. Remove the bacon, and reserve the drippings. Brown the meat in the bacon drippings. Add the chopped onions and cook until clear. Add the jalapeño peppers. Stir frequently. Add the undrained tomatoes, tomato paste, and seasonings. Simmer for 2 hours, stirring occasionally. In a skillet brown the ground beef. Dice the bacon, and add the ground beef and bacon to the chili mixture. Stir thoroughly. Add the beans and heat through. Stir well, and it is ready to serve.
Serves 8.

Hal Kennedy—Nashville, Tennessee

Howard's Scalp Level Chili

My grandmother was born sometime around 1855 in Scalp Level, Pennsylvania. Here is her old-time recipe for what was then called chili soup. I call it Scalp Level Chili and have cut the recipe down to accommodate four moderate eaters if you accompany it with lots of good, crusty bread and a nice green salad. It is more a kind of tasty but semi-cautious Howard Sprague–type chili. Also, while it can be thrown together quite quickly, it should simmer for about an hour and a half, so it is not a recipe that Howard would rush home from the office to cook. He would make it on a Friday evening or a Saturday afternoon, cooking it on top of the stove in his Dutch oven.

1 pound lean ground beef
1 large yellow onion, chopped medium coarse
3 to 4 medium ribs celery, sliced
1/2 green pepper, chopped
3 medium tomatoes, skinned and chopped (or 1 15-ounce can tomatoes)

1/2 cup water
1 15-ounce can kidney beans
1/4 teaspoon finely ground pepper
3 tablespoons chili powder
1 tablespoon brown sugar

In a stock pot or Dutch oven, brown the ground beef. If the meat is very lean, add some oil to the pan before browning. Add the chopped onion, celery, and green pepper, mixing them well with the meat. Add the tomatoes, water, and the liquid from the kidney beans. Stir in the pepper, chili powder, and brown sugar, and bring to a boil. Reduce the heat, cover, and simmer over a low flame for 30 to 40 minutes, when the fat will have risen to the top. Spoon off the fat, add the kidney beans, and replace the cover. Simmer for 40 minutes or more. The longer it cooks, the better it seems to be.

If you like it thick, remove the lid for a while. If you like more liquid, add some water or tomato juice. You may leave out the green pepper if you like, or perhaps add a couple of finely chopped cloves of garlic. Throw in some oregano if you like. Play around with it. Follow Howard's lead and be adventurous.

Serves 4 to 6.

Jack Dodson—cast member

> **BEE:** Do you like pearly onions?
> **BRISCOE:** Oh, they twang my buds.

Busy bee

Ernest T. Bass

For a mountain-grown person, rock-throwing Ernest T. is a pretty picky eater. That's probably because he learned to wash his food from the raccoon he shares a cave with.

As clever and good-looking as he is, Ernest T. has trouble getting and keeping a girl. But those are the breaks—especially when there's a window around. And if he ever tells you, "It's me, it's me, it's Ernest T.," be sure to listen because he doesn't chew his cabbage twice.

Salads

Bannertown Broccoli Salad

3/4 cup mayonnaise
3 tablespoons sugar
3 tablespoons red wine vinegar
2 bunches broccoli, chopped

8 strips bacon, cooked and crumbled
1 cup shredded cheddar cheese
1 red onion, chopped

In a small bowl combine the mayonnaise, sugar, and vinegar. Chill the dressing for at least 1 hour before serving.

In a salad bowl layer the broccoli, bacon, cheese, and onion. Pour the dressing over the salad, and toss before serving.

Serves 6.

Robin and Tommy Ford—Northport, Alabama

Bee's Broccoli Salad

No beating around the bush—it's delicious!

1 cup mayonnaise or salad dressing
2 tablespoons red cider vinegar
1/4 to 1/3 cup sugar
1 bunch broccoli, broken into florets

1/2 cup chopped pecans
1/2 cup chopped red onion
1/2 cup raisins (or any dried fruit)
8 to 10 slices bacon, cooked and crumbled

Combine the mayonnaise, vinegar, and sugar. Cover and refrigerate overnight.

Just before serving, combine the remaining ingredients. Pour the dressing over the salad and mix well. Serve chilled.

Serves 4 to 6.

Freida Crawley—Nashville, Tennessee

Cesar Romero's Lawn Salad

Romaine lettuce
1 clove garlic, minced
Salt and pepper to taste
Pinch thyme and oregano
2 teaspoons lemon juice
1 tablespoon German mustard
$1/2$ tablespoon steak sauce

$1/2$ tablespoon Worcestershire sauce
1 egg
6 tablespoons olive oil
1 tablespoon wine vinegar
$1/2$ cup grated Parmesan cheese
1 cup crustless French bread cubes
1 ounce anchovies

Rinse and dry the lettuce leaves and arrange in a salad bowl. Remove any coarse ribs from the lettuce. Combine the garlic, salt, pepper, thyme, oregano, lemon juice, mustard, steak sauce, Worcestershire sauce, egg, olive oil, and vinegar. Pour over the lettuce and toss. Top with Parmesan cheese, croutons, and anchovies.

Serves 4 to 6.

Elfie's Wilted Lettuce Salad

2 slices cooked bacon, crumbled
$1/4$ cup vinegar

$1/4$ cup sugar
1 small head lettuce, torn

In a saucepan combine the bacon, vinegar, and sugar. Heat through. Place the lettuce in a serving bowl and pour the dressing mixture over the lettuce. Pour the dressing back into the saucepan and heat again. Pour the heated dressing over the lettuce again. Serve.

Serves 4 to 6.

Elfie Johnson—Albuquerque, New Mexico

Ernest Toss Salad

Wild things.

1 head lettuce
$1/2$ cup grated carrots
$1/4$ cup chopped radishes
$1/4$ cup snipped parsley
$1/2$ cup chopped celery
$1/4$ cup chopped green pepper
$1/4$ cup chopped stuffed green olives

$1/2$ cup chopped tomatoes
$1/4$ cup sliced green onions
4 teaspoons Parmesan cheese
4 teaspoons cooked bacon, crumbled
Italian dressing
$1/2$ cup seasoned croutons

Core the lettuce and tear into chunks. Combine all of the ingredients except the croutons in a large bowl and toss well. Add the croutons just before serving.

Serves 6.

Toss and Turn Salad

1 package fresh spinach (about 1 pound)
2/3 cup Bibb lettuce
1 9-ounce can sliced water chestnuts, drained
3/4 cup cooked bacon, crumbled
1/2 cup oil
1/4 cup sugar
1/4 cup chili sauce

2 tablespoons red wine vinegar
1/2 teaspoon Worcestershire sauce
1 small onion, chopped
1/2 teaspoon dry mustard
1/2 teaspoon salt
1/4 teaspoon cayenne pepper
1 hard-boiled egg, grated

In a salad bowl toss together the spinach, lettuce, water chestnuts, and bacon. In a medium bowl combine the oil, sugar, chili sauce, vinegar, Worcestershire sauce, onion, dry mustard, salt, and cayenne pepper. Just before serving, pour the dressing over the salad. Sprinkle with grated egg.

Serves 8.

Spinach Salad Sprague

Great with spaghetti dinners.

1 pound spinach
1 medium red onion, sliced
3 to 5 strips cooked bacon, crumbled
1/4 pound sliced mushrooms (optional)
1/2 cup oil

3/4 cup sugar
1/2 cup catsup
1/2 cup cider vinegar
1 teaspoon salt

Wash and dry the spinach. Cut into bite-sized pieces. In a large salad bowl combine the spinach, onion, bacon, and mushrooms. In a separate bowl combine the remaining ingredients, blending thoroughly. Pour over the salad and serve immediately.

The dressing will keep in the refrigerator for up to 2 weeks.

Serves 6.

Mary Clark—Nashville, Tennessee

Smile with Pyle

Tomatoes Mayberry Marinade

8 tomatoes
2 cloves garlic, minced
1/2 teaspoon salt
1/4 cup oil

2 tablespoons wine vinegar
1 teaspoon oregano
1/4 teaspoon pepper

Dip the tomatoes into boiling water for a few seconds, and then remove the skins. They should peel easily.

Combine the remaining ingredients and pour over the peeled tomatoes. Cover and refrigerate for at least 12 hours.

Place the tomatoes on individual lettuce beds and garnish with minced green onion stems.

Serves 8.

Sue Concelman—Houston, Texas

Toober Beanie Salad

Fill 'er up!

1 16-ounce can red kidney beans
1 16-ounce can yellow wax beans
1 16-ounce can green beans
1 16-ounce can small green peas
1 large red onion, chopped
2 cups red cabbage, shredded

1 7-ounce jar pimento
1/2 cup oil
1 teaspoon salt
1 cup brown sugar
1/2 cup vinegar

Drain all of the beans and the peas, and combine in a large bowl. Add the remaining ingredients. Mix well and cover. Refrigerate for about 12 hours. Stir occasionally. Drain before serving.

Serves 8.

Cecilia Farrar—Browns Summit, North Carolina

Aunt Myrl's Three-Bean Salad

1 16-ounce can cut green beans, drained
1 16-ounce can cut wax beans, drained
1 16-ounce can red kidney beans, drained
1/2 cup diced bell pepper
4 to 5 green onions, finely chopped
1 teaspoon salt

1 teaspoon pepper
3/4 cup sugar
2/3 cup vinegar
2 tablespoons oil
1 tablespoon olive oil

In a large bowl combine the beans, bell pepper, and onion. Sprinkle with salt and pepper, and allow to stand for a few minutes. Add the sugar, and let the mixture stand for a few more minutes. Add the remaining ingredients, toss until well mixed, and chill for several hours or overnight.

Serves 6.

Myrl Sisk—Albuquerque, New Mexico

Briscoe observes Aunt Bee:
BRISCOE: That's the cleanest cookin' woman as I ever did see.
ANDY: Aunt Bee believes cleanliness is next to godliness.
BRISCOE: That's a combination hard to come by. Neat and reverent.

Old Sam's Better Potato Salad

Will get many a nibble.

15 red potatoes	1 1/2 teaspoons vinegar
5 medium eggs	Salt and pepper to taste
1 1/2 tablespoons dried onion (optional)	1 1/4 cups low-fat mayonnaise

In a large pot boil the potatoes over medium heat for 35 to 45 minutes. Boil the eggs over medium heat for 15 minutes. Drain the water from the potatoes and the eggs, and allow both to cool. Chop the potatoes and eggs into a large bowl. Add the dried onion. Add the vinegar. Season with salt and pepper. Gently stir in the mayonnaise. Cover and refrigerate, or eat while warm if preferred.

> *Serves 10.*

Pearl Burgess Murray—Maiden, North Carolina

Picnic Potato Salad

What they like by the lake.

6 medium potatoes, diced	1 onion, chopped
1 rib celery, chopped	1/2 teaspoon celery seed (optional)
1 carrot, chopped	4 tablespoons salad dressing
1 sweet pepper, chopped	1 tablespoon mustard
4 to 5 small sweet pickles, chopped	Paprika

Cook the diced potatoes, and drain. Set aside to cool. When the potatoes are cooled, add the chopped vegetables. Sprinkle with celery seed. Add the salad dressing and mustard, and blend. Sprinkle paprika over the salad.

> *Serves 6 to 8.*

Anita Pruitt—Lebanon, Tennessee

Warren Ferguson

Boston-born Warren Ferguson has tough shoes to fill when he replaces Barney Fife as Mayberry's second in command of law enforcement. There's no doubt, however, that he is well trained for the job. After all, he graduated fourth in his class at the sheriff's academy.

Not only that, but Warren has had experience in the wholesale fish business and is a big fan of Perry Mason. In any case, Warren doesn't stay in Mayberry long. While he is in town, though, he is thoroughly conscientious. As he says, "Efficiency is a deputy's duty."

Granny's Slaw

Great for picnics and all occasions.

1 teaspoon salt
1/4 teaspoon pepper
1/2 teaspoon dry mustard
1/2 teaspoon celery seed
2 tablespoons sugar
1/4 cup chopped green pepper

1 tablespoon pimento
1/2 teaspoon grated onion
3 tablespoons oil
1/3 cup vinegar
3 cups chopped or grated cabbage

In a large bowl combine all of the ingredients. Chill thoroughly.
   Serves 6.

Nellie Fitch—Springfield, Missouri

Cole Porter's Three-Fruit Coleslaw

Something special to Thelma Lou.

1 small cabbage, shredded
1 small carrot, shredded
1 8-ounce can pineapple tidbits, drained

1/4 cup raisins
1/4 cup flaked coconut
1/3 to 1/2 cup mayonnaise

In a large bowl combine all of the ingredients except the mayonnaise. Cover and chill. Just before serving, stir in the mayonnaise.
   Serves 6 to 8.

Winter Wonder Coleslaw

This may be white, but it's no snow job.

3 to 4 raw turnips, peeled and grated
2 ribs celery, diced
8 radishes, sliced
1/2 teaspoon salt

1 green pepper, diced
1/4 cup fat-free Italian dressing
2 tablespoons reduced-calorie mayonnaise
Dash garlic powder

In a serving bowl combine the ingredients in the order given. Chill. Add salt, if desired.
   Serves 4.

Suzanne Chappin—Hendersonville, Tennessee

Gomer Pyle

Filling station attendant Gomer Pyle is one of the few Mayberry men who actually cooks his own meals. That's because his employer, Wally, generously supplies him with a kitchenette in his room in back of the garage. It comes complete with a two-burner stove, an icebox, wooden egg crates, forks, and salt and pepper.

The friendly Gomer has a sweet tooth just like Opie. He loves soda pop straight from the filling station's cooler, as well as peppermint candy from Pearson's Sweet Shop. The lucky boy really hits it big when he joins the U.S. Marine Corps because ("surprise, surprise") he discovers the chow at the mess hall is better than his own cooking.

Garden Club Chicken Salad

2½ cups diced cooked chicken
1 cup finely cut celery
1 cup seedless grapes
1 cup finely chopped nuts
1 teaspoon minced onion

1 teaspoon salt
¾ to 1 cup mayonnaise or salad dressing
½ cup heavy cream, whipped
Crisp lettuce or other greens
Olives, sweet pickle gherkins for garnish

In a large bowl combine the chicken, celery, grapes, nuts, onion, salt, mayonnaise, and cream. Chill. Serve on lettuce or greens, and garnish with olives and pickles.
  Serves 6.

Tuna Taylor Salad

Served at least once a week at the Taylor household.

1 6½-ounce can tuna, drained and flaked
½ cup shredded Swiss cheese
½ cup chopped celery
2 tablespoons finely chopped onion

¼ cup mayonnaise
¼ cup sour cream
Dash pepper
16 slices rye bread

In a bowl combine the tuna, cheese, celery, onion, mayonnaise, sour cream, and pepper. Spread on the bread and serve at once.
  Makes 8 sandwiches.

Sherry Hyatt—Kingsport, Tennessee

On the sidewalk by Main Street:
BARNEY: Uh . . . oh (watching sign painter working on grocery store window).
  ANDY: What's the matter?
BARNEY: Ain't "chicken" spelled "i-n"?
  ANDY: No, he's got it right.
BARNEY: You sure?
  ANDY: Uh-huh. "I" before "e" except after "c," and "e" before "n" in "chicken."
BARNEY: Aw, yeah . . . I always forget that rule.

Myrtle's Melon Balls

1 cantaloupe, scooped into balls
1/4 watermelon, scooped into balls
1 honeydew melon, scooped into balls
2 cups strawberries, washed and halved
2 cups blueberries, washed

1/2 cup sour cream or yogurt
1/2 cup confectioners' sugar or honey
1/2 cup orange juice
2/3 cup chopped pecans

In a large bowl combine the fruits. In a separate bowl combine the remaining ingredients. Pour the dressing over the fruit, and refrigerate for at least 1 hour.
Serves 12.

Watermelon Wally

1/2 cup sugar
1/3 cup light rum

3 tablespoons lime juice
6 cups cubed watermelon

In a small bowl combine the sugar, rum, and lime juice. Place the watermelon in a serving dish and pour the rum mixture over all. Cover and chill for 2 to 3 hours.
Serves 6.

Bee's Bingo Cherry Salad

A sure winner at the Ladies' Auxiliary Luncheon.

2 3-ounce packages cherry gelatin
2 cups boiling water
1 20-ounce can crushed pineapple
1 21-ounce can cherry pie filling
1 8-ounce package cream cheese

1/2 cup sugar
1/2 cup sour cream
1 teaspoon vanilla extract
1/2 cup chopped nuts

In a large bowl combine the gelatin and hot water. Add the pineapple and cherry pie filling. Pour into an 8 x 10-inch glass dish. Chill until set.

Soften the cream cheese and mix well with the sugar. Blend in the sour cream and vanilla. Spread over the gelatin mixture. Sprinkle with nuts.
Serves 6.

Mrs. Frank Brower—Asheboro, North Carolina

Eleanora Poultice A+ Fruit Salad

Sounds delicious—and is!

2 cups diced pineapple
2 cups diced oranges
1/2 cup diced apple
2 bananas, sliced
Miniature marshmallows to taste
2 eggs

1/4 cup sugar
3 tablespoons orange juice
3 tablespoons pineapple juice
2 tablespoons lemon juice
1/2 cup whipping cream, whipped

In a serving bowl carefully combine the diced pineapple, oranges, apple, banana slices, and as many marshmallows as you like.

Beat the eggs well, add the sugar, and beat until blended. Add the juices and mix well. Cook the mixture in the top of a double boiler over low heat until the consistency of custard. Chill.

Drain the liquid from the fruit mixture. Fold the whipped cream into the dressing mixture and mix with the fruit and marshmallow mixture.

Serves 12.

Helen Sisk Van Atta—Albuquerque, New Mexico

Newton's Gelatin Salad

You don't even have to be "ept" to make this one.

1 20-ounce can crushed pineapple
1 3-ounce box lemon gelatin
1 3-ounce box orange gelatin
2 cups boiling water

1 tablespoon vinegar
1/2 teaspoon salt
1 cup grated raw carrots
1/3 cup chopped walnuts

Drain and measure the juice from the pineapple. Add water if necessary to make 2 cups. Set aside. Dissolve the lemon and orange gelatin in the boiling water. Add the vinegar, salt, and reserved pineapple juice. Refrigerate for 30 minutes, or until slightly thickened. Stir in the pineapple, carrots, and walnuts. Chill until set.

Serves 6.

Ada Baddeley—Montreal, Quebec

BARNEY: Did you know that knitters and crocheters seldom have stomach disorders?

Floyd's Fruit and Nut Salad

2 kiwi fruit
2 cups strawberries
2 bananas
1 cantaloupe
1 honeydew melon

1 1/2 cups firm, picked-over blueberries
3/4 cup raisins
1 1/2 cups pecans
1 1/2 cups seedless grapes

Wash the fruit. Slice the kiwis, strawberries, and bananas into a bowl. Scoop out the cantaloupe and honeydew melon with a melon baller. Add the remaining ingredients, cover, and refrigerate until chilled.

Serves 10 or more.

Deborah Brogden—Matthews, North Carolina

Aunt Rebecca's Salad

Yell "Uncle" if you want more!

1 8-ounce can crushed pineapple, juice
    reserved
1 3-ounce package lemon gelatin
1 3-ounce package cream cheese or
    Neufchatel, softened

1 cup whipped cream
Lettuce
Mayonnaise

Measure the pineapple juice, and add water if needed to make 1 cup. Bring to a boil. Add the gelatin, remove from the heat, and stir until dissolved. Allow the mixture to thicken, and then add the crushed pineapple. Fold in the cream cheese and whipped cream. Stir thoroughly and blend until smooth, with no chunks of cream cheese. Pour into a 9-inch square pan and refrigerate for 2 hours. Cut into squares and serve on lettuce, topped with dollops of mayonnaise.

Serves 6.

Elfie Johnson—Albuquerque, New Mexico

The secret to Clara's blue ribbon pickles:
CLARA: Well, I think you'll like them. They're sort of special. This year I went wild with
    allspice.
ANDY: Oh-oh, Miss Johnson, I would have never thought it of you.

Cranberry Sauce Crump

Even turkeys earn straight A's with this sauce.

1 6-ounce package raspberry gelatin
2 cups boiling water
1 16-ounce can whole cranberry sauce
1 8-ounce can crushed pineapple packed in
  its own juice

3/4 cup port wine
1/2 cup cran-orange sauce
1/4 cup chopped walnuts or pecans
1/4 cup chopped celery (or omit, and add
  more nuts)

Dissolve the gelatin in the boiling water. Stir in the cranberry sauce, undrained pineapple, port wine, and cran-orange sauce. Chill until partially set, and fold in the walnuts and celery. Pour into a mold and chill until firm.
  Serves 8 to 10.

Nancy Clark—Greensboro, North Carolina

Frenchy Dressing

Un-believable—count on it!

1 1/2 cups olive oil
2 tablespoons lemon juice
2 tablespoons tarragon vinegar
3 teaspoons onion juice
3 tablespoons finely chopped parsley
1 clove garlic

1 teaspoon salt
1 tablespoon sugar
1 teaspoon celery seed
1 teaspoon mustard seed
1 1/2 cups thick sour cream
Chives

In a glass jar combine all of the ingredients. Chill. Shake well before using.
  Makes about 3 cups.

Homemade Thousand Island Dressing

5 to 6 tablespoons vinegar
1 cup evaporated milk
3 hard-boiled eggs, chopped
1 1/2 cups salad dressing
1 small onion, finely chopped

4 tablespoons sweet pickle relish
3 tablespoons catsup
2 to 3 tablespoons sugar
Dash paprika

In a large bowl combine the vinegar and milk, and set aside to thicken. Add the remaining ingredients, blending well. Store unused dressing in the refrigerator, and use within 2 to 3 days.
  Makes 1 quart.

Uh-oh!

Virgil Vinaigrette

4 medium cloves garlic, crushed
1/2 cup plus 2 tablespoons red wine vinegar
1/2 cup plus 2 tablespoons oil
1/2 teaspoon salt
1/2 teaspoon pepper
Pinch celery salt

1/2 teaspoon dry mustard
1/2 teaspoon dill weed
1/2 teaspoon oregano
1/2 teaspoon basil
2 small scallions, minced
1 tablespoon lemon juice

In a container with a tight-fitting lid combine all of the ingredients. Mix well.
   Makes 1 1/2 cups.

Russian Dressing

3/4 cup mayonnaise
1 hard-boiled egg, finely chopped
1 tablespoon chopped green pepper
1 tablespoon chopped pimento

1 tablespoon chopped chives
1/3 cup chili sauce
Juice of 1/4 lemon

In a jar combine all of the ingredients. Chill.
   Makes about 1 cup.

CUPBOARD QUIZ

1. Who in Mayberry (besides Aunt Bee) makes intoxicating preserves?
   Answer: Jennifer and Clarabelle—the Morrison sisters
2. In what two cities does Andy have the opportunity to eat escargots?
   Answer: Raleigh and Hollywood
3. What flavor was Aunt Bee's ice cream that inspired Cousin Bradford J. Taylor?
   Answer: Strawberry
4. Who in Mayberry has the nickname "cream puff"?
   Answer: Barney-parney-poo
5. According to Goober, where can you get the best mashed potatoes in Mayberry?
   Answer: The Diner

Good news

Grits, Eggs, and Cheese

Betty's Breakfast Grits Casserole

6 cups boiling water
1½ cups grits (prepared according to package directions)
2 teaspoons salt

¾ cup margarine
1 pound sharp cheddar cheese, grated
3 eggs, beaten
Tabasco sauce, a hefty shot

In a saucepan prepare the grits according to the package directions, using 6 cups of water. In an ovenproof dish combine all of the ingredients, mixing well.

Bake in a 250° oven for 1 hour.

Harvey Bullock—writer

Mr. McBeevee's Make-Ahead Breakfast

There's nothing make-believe about this.

1 pound hot sausage
6 slices bread, cubed
1 cup grated cheddar cheese, or more
6 eggs

2 cups milk
1 teaspoon salt, or to taste
1 teaspoon mustard

In a skillet crumble and cook the sausage until browned. Drain. Grease a 9 x 13-inch Pyrex pan and line the bottom with cubed bread. Top with sausage and cheese. In a bowl combine the eggs, milk, and seasonings. Beat well and pour over the layers in the pan. Cover and refrigerate overnight.

Bake in a 350° oven for 30 minutes or until egg mixture cooks through and sets. Cut into squares and serve.

Serves 6 to 8.

Mrs. Frank Brower—Asheboro, North Carolina

Rafe Hollister

As one of Mayberry's leading moonshiners, Rafe considers himself an artist. His preferred genre is the still life. One time when Andy and Barney drop in for a raid, Rafe begs them not to destroy his "masterpiece" still.

Rafe also knows his way around a dinner table. Overall, he finds that Aunt Bee's chicken and dumplings and sweet tater pie make it worth surrendering to the local law. Though life in the hills is where Rafe's happiest, he still likes to visit town every once in a while to take his shot at singing.

Hugo Hopfleisch's German Pizza

1^1/$_2$ cups fat
3 medium potatoes
Salt and pepper
1 7-ounce can Spam, cut into strips
^{1}/$_2$ cup chopped onion

^{1}/$_2$ cup chopped green pepper
3 eggs, beaten
Milk
^{1}/$_2$ cup shredded cheddar cheese

Melt the fat in a large skillet. Pare and slice the potatoes. Spread half of the potatoes in the skillet. Sprinkle with salt and pepper. Arrange half of the Spam strips over the potatoes in spoke fashion. Add another layer of potatoes, the onion, green pepper, and Spam strips. Cover and cook over low heat for about 20 to 30 minutes. Beat the eggs with a small amount of milk. Pour the eggs over all. Cover and cook until the eggs are set, about 10 minutes. Top with cheese. Cover and cook until the cheese melts.

Serves 4 to 6.

Lois Concelman—Houston, Texas

Opie's Row of Spinach Quiche

1 10^1/$_2$-ounce can cream of mushroom soup, undiluted
1 3-ounce package cream cheese
4 eggs
^{3}/$_4$ cup grated Swiss cheese
^{1}/$_2$ package smoky link sausages (or ^{1}/$_2$ cup chopped ham)

1 10-ounce package frozen chopped spinach, cooked and drained
^{1}/$_4$ cup finely chopped green onion
^{1}/$_2$ teaspoon hot sauce
1 unbaked 10-inch pie shell

In a blender or food processor, combine all of the ingredients except the pie shell. Pour the blended mixture into the pie shell. Bake in a 425° oven for 10 minutes. Reduce the temperature to 350° and bake for 35 to 45 minutes, until done. The filling should be set, slightly browned on top, and a knife inserted in the center comes out clean.

Serves 6 to 8.

Mary Jane Hamilton—Houston, Texas

ANDY: If I ever catch a certain little boy handcuffing another little boy to a flagpole, he'll not only be a-plantin' spinach, he'll be eatin' it—standin' up.

Minuteman Quiches

A ready answer at your service.

1 cup margarine, softened
2 3-ounce packages cream cheese, softened
2 cups all-purpose flour
2 2¹/₄-ounce cans deviled ham
1 medium onion, chopped
2 teaspoons margarine

¹/₂ cup grated American or Swiss cheese
2 eggs, slightly beaten
¹/₂ cup milk
1¹/₈ teaspoons nutmeg
Dash pepper

Cream together 1 cup of margarine and the cream cheese until light and fluffy. Gradually add the flour, making a smooth dough. Chill thoroughly.

Shape the dough into 1-inch balls, and then press into twenty-four 1⁷/₈-inch muffin cups. Spoon a small amount of deviled ham into each cup.

Sauté the onion in 2 teaspoons of margarine until soft but not brown. Toss with ¹/₄ cup of cheese, and sprinkle over the deviled ham. Combine the remaining cheese, eggs, milk, nutmeg, and pepper and spoon evenly into the cups. Bake in a 450° oven for 10 minutes. Reduce the heat to 350° and bake for 15 minutes, until the filling is set and the tops are golden brown. Serve warm.

Makes 24 miniature quiches.

Stranger's Huevos Rancheros

Gives gunfighters their courage.

4 strips bacon
2 medium onions, chopped
2 medium cans jalapeño peppers, minced

1 28-ounce can tomatoes
1 cup grated longhorn cheese
8 eggs

In a heavy skillet or Dutch oven fry the bacon. Remove the bacon and reserve the drippings. Sauté the onion in the bacon drippings until clear. Add the peppers, stirring regularly. Add the tomatoes, cutting into smaller pieces with a knife or spatula. Allow the mixture to cook down until most of the liquid has evaporated. Spread grated cheese over the tomatoes, and allow to partially melt. Drop the eggs on top of the mixture. Cover and allow the eggs to poach. Serve immediately, with 2 eggs and a large scoop of tomato mixture on each plate.

This is a great Sunday brunch, with bacon, toast, fruit, and orange juice.
Serves 4.

Hal Kennedy—Nashville, Tennessee

Sly Devil Eggs

6 hard-boiled eggs
1/4 cup melted butter
1/2 teaspoon Worcestershire sauce
1/4 teaspoon dry mustard
1 2 1/2-ounce can deviled ham
3 scallions, minced

1/4 cup butter
1/4 cup all-purpose flour
2 cups milk
Salt and pepper to taste
Grated cheese
English muffins, toasted

Butter a 9-inch square casserole dish. Cut the eggs in half and remove the yolks. Mix the yolks with the melted butter, Worcestershire sauce, mustard, ham, and scallions. Blend until smooth. Stuff the mixture into the egg whites. Arrange the egg halves in the prepared dish.

Melt the remaining butter in a saucepan. Stir in the flour to form a paste and cook for 1 to 2 minutes. Blend in the milk and season to taste. Heat until thickened. Pour the sauce over the eggs and sprinkle with grated cheese. Bake in a 350° oven for 20 to 25 minutes. Serve over toasted English muffins.

Serves 6.

Otis Campbell's Rummy Tummy Omelet

For a high-spirited breakfast.

Make a plain omelet, and place it on a silver-plated dish. Pour 1/2 cup of rum over it, touch a lighted match to it, and serve immediately. Make sure that the rum is of good quality, or it will not burn.

Serves 1.

Alice and Jim Schwenke—Houston, Texas

Helen Crump

Helen made history when she came to Mayberry. She was the first to discover that the quickest way into Andy's heart was not necessarily through his stomach.

As a busy schoolteacher, she simply has little time to perfect her skills in the kitchen. For their dates, she and Andy generally go out to eat at the Diner and maybe take in a movie at the Grand or watch a little TV at her place. Pound for pound, though, dining at Morelli's may be their top choice for a romantic evening.

Nora Belle's Cheese Soufflé

4 tablespoons butter
2 tablespoons flour
1/2 teaspoon salt
Dash cayenne pepper
1 cup scalded milk

1/2 cup or more grated sharp cheddar
  cheese
4 egg yolks, beaten
4 egg whites, beaten stiff

Butter a 1-quart soufflé dish. In a saucepan or double boiler over simmering water, melt the butter. Add the flour and blend well. Add the salt and cayenne. Gradually add the scalded milk. Cook, stirring constantly, until thick and smooth. Add the cheese and stir until the cheese is melted and the sauce is smooth. Remove from the heat and add the egg yolks. Blend well and allow to cool. Fold in the stiffly beaten egg whites. Turn the mixture into the prepared soufflé dish, and set in a pan of hot water. Bake in a 325° oven for 45 minutes to 1 hour, depending on how moist you wish the soufflé to be.

Serves 3 to 4.

Eudora Garrison—Charlotte, North Carolina

Golden Door Baked Macaroni and Cheese

Geronimo!

1/4 cup butter
1/4 cup all-purpose flour
2 1/2 cups milk
1/2 teaspoon salt
1/2 teaspoon dry mustard

1/4 teaspoon pepper
1 teaspoon Worcestershire sauce
2 cups grated sharp cheddar cheese
7 ounces bite-size macaroni, cooked

In a large saucepan melt the butter. Blend in the flour. Gradually add the milk, stirring constantly. Add the seasonings. Cook until the sauce is thickened. Add 1 cup of cheese and stir until melted. Add the cooked macaroni. Turn the mixture into an 8-inch square baking dish. Sprinkle the top with the remaining grated cheese. Bake in a 375° oven for about 15 minutes. Heat under the broiler until the cheese is bubbly and lightly browned.

Serves 4 to 6.

Knot-Tying Club Noodles

Knot bad at all.

1 5-ounce package fine noodles
1 cup cottage cheese
1 cup sour cream
1 clove garlic, minced

1 onion, chopped
1 tablespoon Worcestershire sauce
Dash Tabasco sauce
Salt to taste

Butter a casserole dish. In a large pot cook the noodles in boiling salted water for 10 minutes. Drain. In the prepared dish combine the remaining ingredients, and add the noodles. Toss until coated. Bake in a 350° oven for 45 minutes.

Serves 6.

"Nip it in the bud!"

Mt. Pilot Pimento Cheese Sandwich Spread

10 ounces sharp cheddar cheese, grated
1/2 cup very finely chopped green olives
1/4 cup minced pimentos

1/2 cup mayonnaise
Dash Worcestershire sauce

In a large bowl combine all of the ingredients and mix well. Refrigerate until ready to use.
  Variation: Add 1/2 cup of finely chopped pecans.
  Makes about 2 1/2 cups.

Hogette Winslow's Hogshead Cheese

5 gallons well water
1 whole hog's head, cleaned
5 large onions
Parsley and shallots

1 clove garlic
2 red peppers, finely cut
1 tablespoon black pepper
Salt to taste

In a large kettle bring the water to a boil. Add the hog's head, and boil for 3 hours. Test with a fork to see if it can be pulled apart easily. If not, continue to boil until tender. Remove the head from the liquid, place on a large platter, and remove the bones and skin. Shred the meat, making sure all the small parts of bone have been removed. Return the shredded meat to the kettle.
  Chop the onions, parsley, shallots, and garlic very finely. Add to the kettle and boil for 10 minutes. Add the red pepper, black pepper, and salt. Boil for 1 hour, stirring frequently to prevent sticking and burning. Taste, and add more seasoning if desired. Pour into small glass bowls to serve.
  Serves 6.

Alice and Jim Schwenke—Houston, Texas

Otis reacts to the breakfast served him at the courthouse:
  OTIS: Say, that food smells pretty good. I could never get anything like this at home.
  ANDY: Sure you could. I bet your wife'd fix you a nice *big* breakfast if you'd go up to her in the morning and give her a great big kiss.
  OTIS: Please, Andy, not while I'm eating!

Goober Pyle

Goober is easily Mayberry's least finicky eater. The fact is, he'll eat just about anything within his reach. That includes strawberry ice cream with pickles and a peanut butter and tuna sandwich garnished with catsup. The gobbling Goober is also the town's biggest eater. In fact, one year he distinguished himself by eating 57 pancakes at the county fair, and that includes syrup and butter. Yo!

A true outdoorsman, Goober loves to hunt and fish. Those are his favorite pastimes after he gets off work at the filling station, a job he takes over when cousin Gomer leaves town. Among Goober's favorite foods are mashed potatoes, corn on the cob, and pounded steak. It's a safe bet that not much of anything lays on his chest.

Breads

Ange's Apple Bread

You just have to have some.

2 cups sugar
1 cup oil
3 eggs
3 cups all-purpose flour
1 teaspoon salt

1 teaspoon baking soda
1 teaspoon cinnamon
2 teaspoons vanilla extract
2 cups chopped peeled apples
1 cup nuts

Grease 2 loaf pans. In a large bowl beat together the sugar, oil, and eggs. In a separate bowl sift together the flour, salt, baking soda, and cinnamon. Add the dry ingredients to the sugar mixture. Add the vanilla, apples, and nuts. Pour the batter into the prepared pans. Bake in a 325° oven for 1 hour.
Makes 2 loaves.

Sherry Walls—Collierville, Tennessee

Gomer's Banana Bread Pyle

1 cup butter or oil
2 cups sugar
4 eggs, beaten well
6 to 7 bananas, mashed

2$\frac{1}{2}$ cups sifted all-purpose flour
1 teaspoon salt
2 teaspoons baking soda
$\frac{1}{2}$ cup chopped macadamia nuts

Grease and flour 2 large loaf pans or 5 small ones. Cream the butter with the sugar. Add the eggs and beat well. Add the mashed bananas, stirring to blend. In a separate bowl sift together the dry ingredients. Fold the dry ingredients into the batter, mixing well. Add the macadamia nuts. Pour the batter into the pans. Bake in a 350° oven for 50 to 60 minutes, or until done.
For muffins, fill 12 muffin cups $\frac{3}{4}$ full and bake in a 350° oven for 35 to 45 minutes.
Makes 2 large loaves, 5 small loaves, or 12 large muffins.

Jim Nabors—cast member

He's a Nut Banana Bread

Barney says that this recipe is "first rate, grade A, number one."

1/2 cup butter, softened
1 cup sugar
2 eggs
3 bananas, mashed
1 cup whole wheat flour

1 cup all-purpose flour
1/2 teaspoon baking soda
1/2 teaspoon vanilla extract
1 cup walnuts

Grease and flour 1 large or 2 small loaf pans. In a large bowl cream together the butter and sugar. Add the eggs, blending well. Add the bananas, flours, baking soda, vanilla, and nuts. Mix well. Pour the batter into the prepared pan. Bake in a 300° oven for 1 hour or until brown.

Makes 1 large or 2 small loaves.

Robin and Tommy Ford—Northport, Alabama

Chief Noogatuck's Cranberry Nut Bread

How delicious.

2 cups all-purpose flour
1/2 teaspoon baking soda
2 tablespoons butter
1 cup sugar
1 egg

1/2 teaspoon salt
3/4 cup orange juice
1 cup chopped cranberries
1/2 cup chopped pecans

Grease and flour a loaf pan. In a large bowl sift together the flour and baking soda. In a separate bowl cream together the butter and sugar, and then beat in the egg and salt. Alternately add the flour and orange juice to the creamed mixture. Mix well after each addition. Fold in the cranberries and pecans. Turn into the prepared pan. Bake in a 350° oven for 1 hour.

Makes 1 loaf.

Johnnie Bucy—Lebanon, Tennessee

ANDY: Oh, hi, Opie. You're just in time to join me and Barney for lunch. Aunt Bee made us some extra-special baloney sandwiches.

Mayberry After Midnight Pumpkin Bread

6 eggs
3 cups sugar
2 cups plus 4 tablespoons oil
1 29-ounce can pumpkin (or 2 16-ounce cans)
4^1/$_2$ cups all-purpose flour

2^1/$_2$ teaspoons baking soda
3 teaspoons baking powder
3 teaspoons vanilla extract
2 teaspoons salt
3 teaspoons cinnamon
3 cups crushed walnuts

Grease and flour five 1-pound coffee cans. In a large bowl beat the eggs. Add the sugar and beat well. Add the oil and pumpkin, mixing well. Add the remaining ingredients, and mix well. Fill the cans equally with the batter. Bake in a 350° oven for 50 to 60 minutes. Turn out onto a cooling rack.

This bread freezes well.

Makes 5 loaves.

Mary Ellis—Albuquerque, New Mexico

Miss Edna's Light Bread

A light classic.

6 cups all-purpose flour
3 tablespoons sugar
1 tablespoon salt
2 large rounded tablespoons lard
1 package active dry yeast

^{1}/$_4$ cup tepid water
1 egg
Lukewarm water to make dough
Melted lard

In a large bowl sift together the flour, sugar, and salt. Work in the lard. In a separate bowl dissolve the yeast in ^{1}/$_4$ cup of tepid water. Add the yeast mixture to the flour mixture, then add the egg. Gradually add enough lukewarm water to make a dough a little stiffer than a roll dough. Turn the dough onto a floured board and knead for 5 to 6 minutes. Place the dough in a large greased bowl, and turn once to grease the surface. Cover and let rise in a warm place until double. Punch down and let rise again until almost double in bulk.

Grease 2 loaf pans. Turn onto a floured board and work lightly, but do not knead. Mold into 2 loaves and place in the prepared pans. Bake in a 325° oven for about 50 minutes. Brush the tops with melted lard and bake for 5 more minutes for a nice brown crust. Remove the loaves immediately from the pans and place on a wire rack to cool. Do not place in a draft, or the crust will crack.

Makes 2 loaves.

Eudora Garrison—Charlotte, North Carolina

Dog chow

Andy sorts through Barney's lunch sack for something to feed a stray dog:

ANDY: Well, you've got three sandwiches in here.

BARNEY: Well, that's right: two for lunchtime and one for late in the day when I get my sinking spell.

ANDY: Well, we'll get you another one.

BARNEY: That's on salt-risin' bread, you know.

ANDY: Well, we'll get one on salt-risin' bread. There you are. (Feeds dog) . . . Now, let's see what else . . . there's a Mister Cooky Bar.

BARNEY: Well, come on now. Don't give him my Mister Cooky Bar. I'll want that later on.

ANDY: Well, why?

BARNEY: Well, a slender, high-spirited person needs his sugar pick-me-up late in the day.

Herbed Garlic Bread

¹/₂ cup butter
¹/₂ teaspoon thyme
¹/₂ teaspoon rosemary
¹/₂ teaspoon oregano
¹/₂ teaspoon basil

1 large loaf French bread
4 cloves garlic, minced
Grated Parmesan cheese
Fresh minced parsley

In a small saucepan combine the butter, thyme, rosemary, oregano, and basil. Heat over low heat until the butter is melted. Slice the bread and generously brush the butter mixture on each slice. Sprinkle with minced garlic, Parmesan cheese, and parsley. Bake in a 475° oven or under the broiler until lightly browned.

Serves 6.

Diner Rolls

³/₄ cup boiling water
1 cup shortening
³/₄ cup sugar
2 packages active dry yeast
¹/₄ cup lukewarm water
3 cups all-purpose flour

2 eggs, well beaten
1 tablespoon salt
1 cup water
3 cups whole wheat flour
Melted butter

In a large saucepan bring to a boil ³/₄ cup of water, the shortening, and sugar, stirring constantly. Cool. In a small bowl dissolve the yeast in ¹/₄ cup of warm water. In a large bowl combine the cooled liquid, the all-purpose flour, eggs, and yeast mixture. Beat well. Add the salt and remaining water, and beat well. Add the whole wheat flour. Refrigerate the dough for several hours or overnight.

Roll out the dough on a very lightly floured surface. Cut the rolls with a biscuit cutter, and dip in melted butter. Fold over and pinch the edges. Let the rolls rise for about 1 hour and 30 minutes. Bake in a 350° oven until golden brown.

Makes 50 to 75 rolls.

George Lindsey—cast member

OPIE: It ain't easy getting a peanut butter and jelly sandwich down dry. Yesterday, I almost choked.

Top security

Security Bank Bread

Closely guarded dough.

1 scant cup sugar	2 cups warm water
3 teaspoons salt	3 eggs, room temperature
1 cup shortening	6½ cups all-purpose flour
1 cup hot water	6½ cups whole wheat flour
2 packages active dry yeast	Softened shortening

In a large bowl cream the sugar, salt, and shortening. Pour the hot water over the mixture, and stir until well blended and dissolved. Cool. In a separate bowl sprinkle the yeast over the lukewarm water, and sprinkle a little sugar over to make the yeast foam more quickly. Beat the eggs. Add the eggs and the yeast mixture to the creamed mixture. Add the flours, mixing well. More or less flour may be needed to make a fairly stiff dough. Turn onto a floured board and knead for 4 or 5 minutes. Place in a greased container and turn once to grease the surface. Cover and let rise in a warm place until double in bulk. Punch down, cover, and allow to rise again about half as long as the first time. Work the dough lightly, and divide into 3 parts.

Grease 3 loaf pans, and place the dough in the pans. Brush the tops with softened shortening, cover, and let rise in a warm place until the loaves have risen well above the tops of the pans. Bake in a 350° oven for about 35 to 45 minutes, until golden brown. Lower the heat to 200° for the last few minutes of baking. Remove from the oven and turn onto a rack. Cover with a towel and cool.

Makes 3 loaves.

Eudora Garrison—Charlotte, North Carolina

Regal Order Rolls

An open door to great taste.

4 to 5 cups all-purpose flour	½ teaspoon salt
2 packages active dry yeast	2 eggs
1 cup milk	4 tablespoons butter or margarine, softened
¾ cup sugar	1 egg, beaten
3 tablespoons butter or margarine	1 tablespoon oil
1 teaspoon finely shredded orange peel	1 tablespoon sugar

In a large bowl combine 2 cups of the flour and the yeast. In a saucepan heat the milk, ¾ cup of sugar, 3 tablespoons of butter, the orange peel, and salt until warm (115° to 120°) and the butter is almost melted. Stir constantly. Add the warm mixture to the flour mixture. Add 2 eggs. Beat with an electric mixer at low speed for 30 seconds, scraping the sides of the bowl constantly. Beat for 3 minutes on high speed. Using a wooden spoon, stir in as much of the remaining flour as possible.

Turn the dough onto a lightly floured surface. Knead in enough of the remaining flour to make a soft dough, kneading for about 3 to 5 minutes. Shape the dough into a ball and place in a greased bowl. Turn the dough to grease the surface. Cover and let rise in a warm place until nearly double, about 45 minutes to 1 hour.

Grease a 10 x 15-inch pan. Punch the dough down and divide in half. Cover and let the dough rest for 10 minutes. Roll each half into a 6 x 12-inch rectangle. Spread each rectangle with 2 tablespoons of the softened butter or margarine. Fold the dough lengthwise into thirds, moisten, and pinch the seam to seal. Flatten slightly and cut crosswise into 1-inch slices. Place the rolls seam-side down in the pan. Cover and let rise until nearly double, about 30 to 45 minutes. Stir together the remaining egg and oil. Brush over the rolls, and sprinkle with sugar. Bake in a 375° oven for 15 to 18 minutes or until done.

Makes 24 rolls.

The Golden Door to Good Fellowship ("Geronimo")

Howard and Andy peruse the menu on a train. Howard insists on buying:

ANDY: You know what I might have? The special—fish cakes. Might just hit the spot.

HOWARD: You know something, Andy? I had my eye on that baby, too.

ANDY: Did you really?

HOWARD: Yeah. You know what I like about fish is it combines a high nutritional value with flavor at a modest price.

ANDY: Can't ask anything more of a fish than that, can you?

HOWARD: Anything to start with?

ANDY: Oh, I don't know. Maybe a roll.

HOWARD: Well, we certainly have the same tastes. I'm a roll man myself.

Helen's Honor Rolls

You'll move to the head of the class with these.

2 packages active dry yeast
1/2 cup warm water
1 cup boiling water
1/2 cup margarine
3/4 cup shortening

2 eggs
2/3 cup sugar
1 cup cold water
7 cups self-rising flour (more if needed)
Melted butter

Dissolve the yeast in the warm water. In a saucepan combine the boiling water, margarine, and shortening, and allow the margarine and shortening to melt. In a large bowl combine the eggs and sugar, and add the cold water. Add the yeast mixture and the melted margarine mixture. Add the flour, adding more flour if needed. Cover and place in the refrigerator until ready to use, 3 to 4 days. Turn onto a floured board and roll out. Cut with a biscuit cutter. Fold each roll over and dip in melted butter. Let the rolls rise in a warm place for 1 hour. Bake in a 400° oven for 10 to 12 minutes.

For a smaller amount, make half of the recipe.

Freida Crawley—Nashville, Tennessee

Quarter Tip Rolls

Best when served by a moody gypsy.

1 1/2 cups all-purpose flour
3/4 cup cornmeal
1 package active dry yeast
1 teaspoon baking powder
3/4 cup milk

1/3 cup shortening
3 tablespoons sugar
1 teaspoon salt
1 egg

In a large bowl combine 3/4 cup of flour, the cornmeal, yeast, and baking powder. In a saucepan heat the milk, shortening, sugar, and salt until just warm enough for the shortening to melt. Add the liquid mixture to the dry ingredients. Beat with an electric mixer at low speed for 30 seconds, scraping the sides of the bowl. Add the egg, and beat at high speed for 3 minutes. Beat in the remaining flour at low speed for 2 minutes, or until smooth. Cover and refrigerate for several hours or overnight.

Stir down the dough, and let rest for 10 minutes. Grease twelve 2 1/2-inch muffin cups, and fill 1/2 full. Cover and set aside to rise for 1 hour, or until doubled. Bake in a 325° oven for 20 to 25 minutes, or until golden brown.

Makes 12 rolls.

Andy and Barney return from lunch at the Diner:

BARNEY: I don't know how they do it for 80 cents.

ANDY: I don't either, I tell you.

BARNEY: Three Vienna sausages—heavy on the tomato puree, slice of bread and butter on a paper dish.

ANDY: And a more than ample portion of succotash. Don't leave out the succotash.

BARNEY: Yeah. You know, when you get a good meal like that with as good a service as Olive gives you, you don't mind leaving a generous tip.

ANDY: Did you leave a tip?

BARNEY: Well, yeah, a quarter.

ANDY: I did, too.

BARNEY: A quarter?

ANDY: Yeah.

BARNEY: Well, Andy, didn't you see me put a quarter down? That was supposed to be for the both of us.

ANDY: Huh. I'll be dogged. Oh, what the heck. It's just a quarter.

BARNEY: Well, no, Andy. That's just throwing money away. Look, I'll just run back over there and put my hat down on one of the quarters and get it back.

ANDY: Barney, that's not necessary. Poor ol' Olive is a widow with four children. She can use it.

BARNEY: Oh, yeah. I forgot about that, bless her heart. (Pauses to contemplate the situation) Let's just let her keep it.

ANDY: You're all heart, you know that, Barn.

The next day:

OLIVE: (To Barney) Say, you and Andy left an extra quarter yesterday. I'm sure it was a mistake.

BARNEY: What do you mean a mistake! That was your tip.

OLIVE: Two quarters? But you never even . . .

BARNEY: Olive! Who do you think you're dealing with? A couple of pikers? You got yourself a half a "C" tip. Enjoy it.

Gertrude's Rowboat Rolls

Try these—oar else.

1/2 cup shortening

1/3 cup sugar

1 cup milk, scalded

1 cup boiling water

1 package active dry yeast

1/4 cup lukewarm water

2 eggs

6 cups self-rising flour

Melted butter

In a large bowl cream the shortening and sugar. Combine the scalded milk and boiling water, and pour over the creamed mixture. Stir until the shortening melts. Cool slightly. In a small bowl dissolve the yeast in 1/4 cup of lukewarm water, adding a pinch of sugar and allowing the mixture to foam. Beat the eggs and add to the yeast mixture. Add the egg mixture to the creamed mixture. Sift the flour and add to the creamed mixture. The dough will be rather loose, and it may be necessary to add more flour. Cover the dough and place in a warm place to rise until doubled in bulk. Punch down, cover, and refrigerate for several hours or overnight.

When ready to make into rolls, punch down again. Turn onto a floured board. Divide the dough into portions and knead a few minutes. Roll to about the thickness of biscuit dough, cut with a biscuit cutter, and brush the surface of each roll with melted butter. Fold in half, press down, and brush the top of each with melted butter.

Grease shallow baking pans or cookie sheets. Arrange the rolls in the prepared pans. Cover and let rise in a warm place until doubled in bulk. Bake in a 450° to 475° oven for about 5 to 6 minutes, until just "set." The tops will not be browned at all. Remove from the oven, cool, and wrap in foil or waxed paper. Refrigerate or freeze. When ready to serve, return to the baking pans, brush with melted butter, and finish baking in a 450° to 475° oven for 5 to 6 minutes.

They may be completely baked the first time, if you're ready to serve them. But this pre-baked idea is wonderful, since the rolls always taste as if they'd just been risen.

Makes 6 to 7 dozen small rolls.

Eudora Garrison—Charlotte, North Carolina

Great-Grandmother Minnie's Rolls

Make many a day.

3 1/2 to 4 cups self-rising flour, sifted
1 package active dry yeast
3 tablespoons warm water
1 cup lukewarm water

6 tablespoons shortening
1/3 cup sugar
1 egg, well beaten

In a bowl sift the flour. In a separate bowl dissolve the yeast in 3 tablespoons of warm water. Add the lukewarm water, shortening, sugar, and egg. Slowly add the flour, blending well. Refrigerate overnight.

Shape the dough into rolls and let the rolls rise in a warm place. Bake in a 350° oven until lightly browned on the top.

Makes about 3 dozen rolls.

Polly Andrews—Gulf Shores, Alabama

Italian Breadsticks

5½ to 6 cups all-purpose flour
2 packages active dry yeast
2 teaspoons salt
2 cups warm water (115° to 120°)

1 slightly beaten egg white
1 tablespoon water
Coarse salt, garlic salt, or Parmesan cheese

In a large bowl combine 2 cups of flour, the yeast, and salt. Add 2 cups of warm water. Beat with an electric mixer at low speed for 30 seconds, scraping the sides of the bowl constantly. Beat at high speed for 3 minutes. With a spoon, stir in as much of the remaining flour as possible. Turn out onto a lightly floured surface and knead in enough of the remaining flour to make a stiff dough that is smooth and elastic, kneading for 8 to 10 minutes. Shape into a ball and place in a greased bowl, turning to grease the surface. Cover and let rise in a warm place until double, about 1 hour to 1 hour and 30 minutes.

Grease a baking sheet. Punch down, turn onto a lightly floured surface, and divide in half. Cover and let rest for 10 minutes. Cut each half into 24 pieces. Roll each piece into a rope 8 inches long. Place the ropes on the baking sheet, cover, and let rise until nearly double, about 30 minutes. Beat the egg white with the water and brush the ropes with the mixture. Sprinkle with coarse salt, garlic salt, or Parmesan. Bake in a 375° oven for 10 minutes. Reduce the temperature to 300° and bake for 20 to 25 minutes longer.

Makes 48 breadsticks.

Raleigh Rolled Dumplings

2 cups all-purpose flour
½ teaspoon baking soda
½ teaspoon salt

3 tablespoons shortening
¾ cup buttermilk

In a large bowl combine the flour, baking soda, and salt. Cut in the shortening until the mixture resembles coarse meal. Add the buttermilk, stirring with a fork until the dry ingredients are moistened. Turn the dough onto a well-floured surface, and knead lightly 4 or 5 times. Roll the dough to ⅛-inch thickness and cut into strips or small squares. Slowly drop the dumplings into boiling broth.

Serves 4 to 6.

Carolina Corn Pone

Nothing could be finer.

1 cup cornmeal (not self-rising)
1 teaspoon salt

1 cup boiling water (more as needed)
2 tablespoons bacon drippings or oil

In a bowl combine the cornmeal and salt. Add the boiling water slowly, stirring to remove the lumps. Add enough water to make a medium batter. Put the bacon drippings or oil on a cookie sheet with sides, and heat it in the oven. Remove the pan from the oven and tilt it from side to side so it is well coated. Then pour the hot drippings into the cornmeal mixture. Stir well. Using a large mixing spoon, drop the batter onto the cookie sheet by the spoonful. Pat a little with the back of the spoon. Bake in a 400° oven for about 25 minutes. The corn pone should be crusty on the bottom and soft in the center.

Serves 4 to 6.

Tonya Hamel—Greensboro, North Carolina

Carlotta Corn Muffins with Cheese and Chilies

1 cup yellow cornmeal
1 cup all-purpose flour
2 tablespoons sugar
1 1/2 teaspoons salt
1 tablespoon baking powder
2 eggs, separated
1/4 cup shortening, melted

2 cups heavy cream
1 cup grated Monterey Jack or jalapeño cheese
3/4 cup corn kernels, drained
1/2 cup diced red bell pepper
1/4 cup diced fresh jalapeño or mild green chilies

Generously butter 12 to 14 small or 28 miniature muffin cups. Preheat the oven to 425° and place the buttered molds on top of the stove to warm.

Combine the cornmeal, flour, sugar, salt, baking powder, egg yolks, melted shortening, and cream in a mixing bowl. Stir in the cheese, corn, bell pepper, and chilies. In a separate bowl beat the egg whites until stiff. Fold the whites into the batter. Spoon into buttered molds. Bake the muffins for 12 to 15 minutes. Watch closely and do not allow the muffins to get too brown. The edges should be golden. Cool for 5 minutes, then run a knife around the edges to loosen the muffins. Turn onto wire racks.

Makes 12 to 14 small or 28 miniature muffins.

Harvey Bullock—writer

Andy and the Darlings

The Darlings

The Darlings are known as a "family of hearty-eating men." Pretty Charlene does most of the grub-making for father Briscoe and brothers Doug, Rodney, Mitch, and Dean up in the mountains.

After Charlene married Dud Wash, the boys tried their hand at cooking, but they just weren't worth a hoot. That's probably why they were all more than happy to pile in the truck and head to Mayberry for some of Aunt Bee's home cooking.

In fact, it was Aunt Bee's cooking that almost won Briscoe's heart. He had spooning on his mind until she spooned him—right smack on the wrist. He soon decided her blueberry muffins just weren't worth the pain.

Blue Ridge Mountain Cornbread

Man does not live by white bread alone.

2 eggs, separated
2 teaspoons sugar
1 cup cornmeal
1 cup milk

1 cup sifted all-purpose flour
2 tablespoons butter, melted
3 teaspoons baking powder
Pinch salt

In separate bowls beat the egg whites and egg yolks. To the egg yolks add the sugar, and beat well. Add the cornmeal, milk, and flour. Add the melted butter, beaten egg whites, baking powder, and salt. Pour into a greased tin pan. Bake in a 450° oven until golden and done, about 15 minutes for an 8-inch square pan. Cut into large squares.

Serves 4 to 6.

Alice and Jim Schwenke—Houston, Texas

True Blueberry Buttermilk Muffins

Detectable delectables.

2^1/$_2$ cups all-purpose flour
2^1/$_2$ teaspoons baking powder
1 cup sugar
^{1}/$_4$ teaspoon salt
1 cup buttermilk

2 eggs, beaten
^{1}/$_2$ cup butter, melted and slightly browned
1^1/$_2$ cups fresh blueberries, rinsed and
   drained

Grease 24 small muffin cups. In a large bowl sift together the dry ingredients. Make a well in the center, and add the buttermilk, eggs, and butter. Mix well. Fold in the blueberries. Pour into the prepared muffin cups. Bake in a 400° oven for 20 minutes.

Makes 24 small muffins.

Ernest T. tries to learn table manners:

OPIE: Mr. Bass, will you pass the bread, please?

ERNEST T.: Uh-huh. Here it is. (Flings a slice to Opie)

AUNT BEE: Mr. Bass, throwing food is a sin!

ANDY: It certainly is. You *pass* it. You don't *throw* it.

ERNEST T.: I just don't cotton to all this. Too doggone many rules. I don't like it. I don't like it.

Bran Muffins Moulage

Will make you an able baker, Charlie.

1 cup 100% bran cereal	2 cups buttermilk
1 cup boiling water	2 1/2 cups all-purpose flour
1 1/4 cups sugar	2 1/2 teaspoons baking soda
1/2 cup shortening	3/4 teaspoon salt
2 eggs	2 cups All-Bran cereal

In a small bowl combine the 100% bran cereal and the boiling water. Set aside to cool. In a separate bowl cream together the sugar and shortening. Add the eggs one at a time to the creamed mixture. Add the buttermilk and 100% bran. Mix together the flour, soda, and salt, and add to the creamed mixture. Stir in the All-Bran cereal. Store in a covered container in the refrigerator until needed. The batter keeps for 2 weeks.

Grease muffin cups and fill 3/4 full. Bake in a 350° oven for 25 minutes.
Makes about 4 dozen muffins.

Betty Martin—Clovis, New Mexico

Barney's Banana Muffins

No slip-ups here.

1 1/2 medium bananas, mashed	1/2 teaspoon baking soda
1/2 cup sugar	1/4 cup oil
1 egg	1 tablespoon water
1 cup self-rising flour	

Grease 12 muffin cups. In a large bowl combine all of the ingredients. Stir just until moistened. Pour the batter into the prepared muffin cups. Bake in a 375° oven for about 10 to 12 minutes.
Makes 1 dozen muffins.

Ada Baddeley—Montreal, Quebec

Fun Girls Pecan Muffins

A real scream.

1 1/2 cups all-purpose flour	1/2 teaspoon salt
1/2 cup sugar	1 egg, slightly beaten
1/2 cup chopped pecans	1/2 cup milk
2 teaspoons baking powder	1/4 cup oil

Grease 12 muffin cups. In a large bowl combine the flour, sugar, pecans, baking powder, and salt. In a small bowl combine the egg, milk, and oil. Make a well in the center of the dry ingredients and pour the milk mixture into the well. Stir just until moistened. Pour the batter into the prepared muffin cups, filling each cup 2/3 full. Bake in a 400° oven for 15 to 20 minutes. Remove from the pan immediately.

Makes 1 dozen muffins.

Hazel Beck—North Little Rock, Arkansas

Thelma Lou's Neighborly Popovers

3 eggs
1 cup milk
1 cup sifted all-purpose flour

1/2 teaspoon salt
1 tablespoon butter or margarine, melted

Grease ten 5-ounce ovenproof custard cups. In a large bowl beat together all of the ingredients with an electric mixer or rotary beater. Pour the batter into the cups, filling them about 1/3 full. Bake in a 400° oven for about 30 minutes, until the popovers are firm, crusty, and golden.

Makes 10 popovers.

Betty Lynn—cast member

Briscoe's Biscuits

"Bread!"

2 cups self-rising flour
1 cup milk

4 tablespoons mayonnaise

In a bowl combine all of the ingredients. Drop onto a greased baking sheet. Bake in a 450° oven until browned.

Makes about 18 biscuits.

Opie asks Andy at the dinner table if they are rich or poor.

ANDY: I'd say we're better off than a lot of people. Got a roof over our heads, Aunt Bee—finest food you ever put in your mouth—Barney for a friend. Yeah, in some ways I'd say we are rich.

BARNEY: You see, Opie, it ain't only the materialistic things in this world that makes a person rich. There's love and friendship. That can make a person rich.

Grandma's Biscuits

These biscuits will pop your eyes out! Mmm, hush.

3 cups self-rising flour
A right smart handful of hog lard
  (or $1/2$ cup shortening)

1 cup milk

Grandma places her flour in a large bowl, makes a well in the center of it, and adds the lard and milk to it. Work it together and roll it out. Cut out small biscuits (a small juice can works well). Bake in a 425° oven until golden brown.

   Makes about 3 dozen biscuits.

Lois Rogers—Readyville, Tennessee

Johnny Paul Jason

Johnny Paul and best friend Opie often swap valuable information. The worldly Johnny Paul is a walking encyclopedia of useful information. For example, he tells Opie that if you lick indelible ink, you die in a minute and a half.

   The wise youngster also gets away with a few things that most Mayberry kids can only dream about—like reading in bed under the covers with a flashlight and owning a No. 1 size chemistry set. If Johnny Paul doesn't exactly keep pace with his companions, perhaps it is because he hears a different drummer. Indeed, all indications are that his is a kid's life that can't be beat.

Mrs. Larch's Denver Biscuits

They'll travel from near and far for these.

1/2 cup mashed white potatoes
1/2 cup shortening
2 cups scalded milk
1 package active dry yeast
1/2 cup lukewarm water

6 cups all-purpose flour, sifted
1/2 cup sugar
1 teaspoon baking powder
1/2 teaspoon baking soda
1 teaspoon salt

In a large bowl combine the potatoes and shortening. Pour scalded milk over the mixture, and blend until the shortening is melted. Cool. In a small bowl dissolve the yeast in the lukewarm water and add to the cooled mixture. Sift together the flour, sugar, baking powder, baking soda, and salt. Add to the potato mixture, stirring to make a soft dough. Cover and let rise in a warm place until doubled in bulk.

Grease baking sheets or shallow pans. Stir down the dough. Turn onto a lightly floured surface, working with half of the dough at a time if desired. Roll the dough out to the thickness of regular biscuits, and cut with a biscuit cutter. Brush with butter and fold over as for pocketbook rolls, or allow to stay in biscuit shapes. Place on the prepared baking sheets and cover. Let the biscuits rise in a warm place until almost doubled.

Bake in a 450° to 475° oven for a few minutes, just until "set" but not brown. Remove from the oven, cool, and wrap well. Freeze the biscuits. When ready to use, brush the pre-baked biscuits with butter and finish baking in a 450° to 475° oven for 5 to 6 minutes, or until golden brown.

Makes 5 to 6 dozen biscuits, depending on size.

Eudora Garrison—Charlotte, North Carolina

OLD LADY CRUMP'S CLASSROOM

1. What night of the week do Barney and Thelma Lou usually eat cashew fudge?
   Answer: Tuesday
2. Who said, "Great beans, Aunt Bee"?
   Answer: Doug Darling
3. Who serves ice cream sundaes with pickles on top?
   Answer: Opie (at Crawford's Drugs)
4. Who eats ice cream sundaes with pickles on top?
   Answer: Goober
5. What is the name of a Chinese restaurant in Mt. Pilot?
   Answer: Either Dave's Hong Kong or Ching Lee's

Aunt Bee's Spoon Bread

Briscoe Darling hollers about this one.

1³/₄ cups boiling water
³/₄ cup sifted cornmeal
2 tablespoons butter
2 eggs (3, if small)

1¹/₄ cups milk
1 teaspoon salt
1 teaspoon baking powder

In the top of a double boiler over simmering water, pour the boiling water over the cornmeal. Stir constantly until thick and smooth, about 5 minutes. Add the butter and blend until melted. Let the mixture cool.

Grease a medium-sized baking dish. Beat the eggs and add the milk and salt. Stir the egg mixture into the cornmeal mixture. Beat until well mixed. Add the baking powder and beat well. Turn into the prepared dish. Bake in a 425° oven for 45 minutes, until firm, but still moist.

Serves 4 to 5.

Eudora Garrison—Charlotte, North Carolina

Boysinger's Bakery Fresh Cinnamon Buns

They'll be fighting over these.

1 cup mashed potatoes
1 cup potato water
³/₄ cup shortening
1 tablespoon salt
3 tablespoons sugar
1 egg
1 package active dry yeast

¹/₂ cup lukewarm water
1 cup milk
5 to 6 cups all-purpose flour
Light brown sugar
Raisins
Cinnamon

In a large bowl combine the mashed potatoes and potato water. Add the shortening, blending well. Add the salt, sugar, and egg. In a small bowl combine the yeast and lukewarm water, stirring until dissolved. Add the yeast mixture to the potato mixture. Add the milk alternately with the flour. Knead the dough, and place in a large bowl. Grease the top of the dough with butter or margarine. Place in the refrigerator overnight.

The next morning, grease two 9 x 13-inch baking pans. Turn the dough onto a floured board. Roll out a large even pastry. In a bowl combine a generous amount of brown sugar, raisins, and cinnamon. Sprinkle the mixture over the dough. Make several large rolls from the pastry, and then cut individual buns from the rolls. Place on the prepared pans. Bake in a 350° oven for 20 minutes. Watch the buns carefully.

Serves 10 to 12.

Mrs. W. J. Edwards—Charlotte, North Carolina

Goober's Pancakes 57

Goober ate 57 of these in one sitting, but you can start with four.

2/3 cup sifted all-purpose flour
1 1/2 teaspoons baking powder
1 1/2 teaspoons sugar
1/4 teaspoon salt

1 egg, beaten
1/2 cup milk
1 tablespoon oil

In a large bowl sift together the dry ingredients. In a separate bowl combine the egg, milk, and oil. Add the egg mixture to the dry ingredients, stirring just until moistened. Bake on a hot, lightly greased griddle.
Makes four 4-inch pancakes.

Freida Crawley—Nashville, Tennessee

Goober talks about the time he ate 57 pancakes with syrup and butter:
GOOBER: I can't eat like that anymore. You want to know what my secret was?
ANDY: Secret for what?
GOOBER: Eating the pancakes.
ANDY: Starved yourself for a week?
GOOBER: That's where you're wrong. The idea is to stuff yourself for a month or two. Stretches your stomach muscles.

Waffles Warren

Gee, men love 'em.

3 eggs
1 cup milk
1/2 teaspoon salt

2 cups sifted all-purpose flour
1 cup melted butter
2 teaspoons baking powder

In a large bowl beat the eggs and blend in the milk. Add the salt and flour, and beat until smooth. Add the melted butter and blend well. Beat in the baking powder until well mixed. Pour the batter onto a hot waffle iron, and bake according to the manufacturer's directions.
Makes about 6 round waffles the size of a breakfast plate.

Eudora Garrison—Charlotte, North Carolina

Leon

There's not much you can say about Leon. Even Leon says nothing about Leon. In fact, Leon says nothing at all. The generous sandwich-eater seems content with his peanut butter and jelly. It's a good thing, too, because he probably receives more repeated rejection ("No thanks, Leon") than anybody else in Mayberry.

Nevertheless, if there's ever trouble, don't let his gentle demeanor fool you. The pistol-packing cowboy might quick-draw more than a sandwich. Enough said.

Little League Egg-Dipped Toast

Batter up!

3 eggs
1/2 teaspoon salt
1 teaspoon sugar

1 cup milk
6 to 8 slices bread, 2 to 3 days old
Butter or margarine

In a shallow dish beat the eggs slightly and add the salt, sugar, and milk. Dip the bread slices in the mixture, turning to moisten both sides. Butter a griddle or skillet well and brown the bread on both sides. Add butter as needed to keep the slices from sticking. Serve hot.

This is very good with bacon or ham and preserves.

Serves 3 to 4.

Leon's Thankless Peanut Butter and Jelly Sandwich

2 slices bread (white is best)
Peanut butter

Jelly (grape is tops)

Spread lots of peanut butter on one side of each piece of bread. This will keep the jelly from soaking through the bread. Put lots of jelly on top of the peanut butter on one slice of bread, and place the other slice of bread peanut butter–side down on top of the jelly. Flip the sandwich over so that the slice of bread with jelly on it is now on top. This allows gravity to pull the jelly down to the peanut butter on the other slice.

Help gravity out by "smooshing" the slices of bread together so that the jelly sort of sticks to the peanut butter. Don't cut the sandwich. It's ready to eat. Just take a bite and offer some to a passerby. (No thank you, Leon.)

OPIE: Mr. Stevens was planning to show us how to make pancakes out of powdered eggs, oatmeal mix, and water over an outdoor fire . . . before we got rained out.

AUNT BEE: Well, as a cook, I think it was fortunate that the rains came when they did.

Peanut Butter Banana Boat

Goober even likes it with catsup.

Peanut butter to taste
1 slice bread, preferably whole wheat
1/2 banana, peeled

8 to 12 raisins (optional)
1 glass cold skim milk (optional)

Spread the peanut butter on the bread. Place the banana diagonally on the bread and roll up the sides. Top with raisins. Wash down with cold milk.
   Serves 1.

David Allen—Birmingham, Alabama

Double duty

Ma Parker's Boardinghouse Cornbread Stuffing

Registers among Raleigh's favorites.

4 teaspoons margarine
1 cup finely diced celery
1/2 cup diced onion
1/2 cup diced green pepper
4 cups crumbled cornbread

2 cups crumbled biscuit or toast crumbs
2 teaspoons dried sage
3 hard-boiled eggs, chopped
2 to 4 cups turkey or chicken broth
Salt and pepper

Grease a 3-quart dish. In a large heavy skillet melt the margarine over medium heat. Sauté the celery, onion, and green pepper until tender. Combine the cornbread, biscuits, and sage, and add to the skillet. Add the chopped eggs. Pour in 2 or more cups of broth, until moistened to taste. Add salt and pepper to taste. Spoon the stuffing into the prepared dish. For moist stuffing, cover and bake in a 350° oven for 40 minutes. For crusty stuffing, cover and bake for 20 minutes, uncover, and bake for 20 minutes more.

Serves 6.

OPIE: Wanna know something, Paw? A sandwich sure tastes better with milk.

"Such goin's-on, such goin's-on."

Barney Fife

Barney is Mayberry's number one deputy and Andy's best friend. With the responsibilities that face him each day in Mayberry's "gateway to danger," he realizes how important it is that he have a proper diet.

Oh, sure, he sometimes junks out on burgers and fries at the Diner or on Mister Cooky Bars and Thelma Lou's cashew fudge. But he never puts on an ounce of fat, except for that time Aunt Bee fattened him up to pass the law enforcement officers' physical exams.

Barney's tastes also lead him to occasional flirting with Juanita, sipping cider with Mrs. Mendelbright, or vacationing in Raleigh where he always enjoys his corner room at the Y and a little late-night tapioca pudding.

Entrees

Ev's Vegetarian Dinner

2 medium red potatoes, boiled and cubed
2 large onions, chopped
1 tablespoon oil
1 10-ounce package frozen green peas, thawed

2 large tomatoes, cut up (or 1 14-ounce can stewed tomatoes)
1 large green pepper, cubed
Spike (or salt and pepper to taste)

In a large pan cook the potatoes and onions in the oil for about 5 minutes. Add everything else and cook for about 5 minutes more.

Serves 4 to 6.

Everett and Deane Ward Greenbaum—writer

Vincente Spaghetti

1 or 2 cloves garlic, minced
3 tablespoons olive oil
1/4 cup snipped parsley
1/4 teaspoon salt

1/8 teaspoon crushed red pepper (optional)
Dash pepper
6 ounces hot cooked spaghetti

In a small saucepan or skillet brown the garlic in the olive oil. Stir in the parsley, salt, red pepper, and pepper. Heat, stirring constantly, for 3 minutes. Remove from the heat and toss with the spaghetti. Serve immediately.

Serves 4.

Apron strings for a bow tie:
> **HOWARD:** That was an excellent dinner, Mother.
> **MRS. SPRAGUE:** Thank you, Howard. Oh, Howard . . . Howard, you've gone back to your father's old habit of not rinsing the backs of the plates.

Meet Barney Fife, big spender:

BARNEY: I remember when I went overboard with Thelma Lou on her last birthday.

ANDY: You get her something nice?

BARNEY: Nicest present I ever gave her. Know what I did?

ANDY: Uh-uh.

BARNEY: Took her out to dinner.

ANDY: Took her out to dinner?

BARNEY: Well, yeah, you know we usually go dutch. Took her to Morelli's.

ANDY: Oh, Morelli's!

BARNEY: Yeah, huh?

ANDY: Yeah.

BARNEY: Yeah. Now there's a place to take a girl. Out on the highway like that, nice and secluded. Red-checkered tablecloths.

ANDY: Oh, yeah, fancy. Fancy.

BARNEY: You know they'll let you take a bottle in there.

ANDY: You didn't, did you?

BARNEY: Na-ah.

ANDY: What'd you have to eat?

BARNEY: They had their Deluxe Special. You know you can hold it down to $1.85 out there if you don't have the shrimp cocktail.

ANDY: Did you have shrimp cocktail?

BARNEY: Well, no. I told Thelma Lou let's not fill up. Minestrone was delicious, though.

ANDY: Oh, yeah, when that's made right, that's really something.

BARNEY: Then for the main dish—pounded steak à la Morelli!

ANDY: Oh.

BARNEY: It's really pounded, too. No question about it. They got one of these open kitchens, and you can look right in there and watch 'em pound it right with your own eyes.

ANDY: Oh, yeah. Kinda see what you're getting.

BARNEY: I tell you, Andy, when that meal was finished, I did something I rarely do.

ANDY: What?

BARNEY: I sent my compliments back to the chef. They appreciate them things. He kinda looked up from his pounding, sort of waved at me.

ANDY: Yeah, I'm gonna have to take Helen over there one of these days.

BARNEY: Oh, she'd love it, lo-ove it! It's not only the food either—it's the atmosphere. You know they got the candles on the table and the music. They got a gypsy violinist out there. He must have played six or eight songs standing over our table. 'Course, you gotta slip him a quarter.

ANDY: Yeah, those fellas work on tips.

BARNEY: One thing about gypsies, though. They're moody.

Pounded Steak à la Morelli

Don't forget to wave to the chef.

1 1/2 pounds round steak
1/4 cup all-purpose flour
1 teaspoon salt
2 tablespoons shortening

1 16-ounce can sliced tomatoes
1/2 cup finely chopped celery
1/2 cup finely chopped carrots
1/2 teaspoon Worcestershire sauce

Cut the steak into 6 portions. Combine the flour and salt, and sprinkle 2 tablespoons of the mixture over the steak. Pound the mixture into both sides of the steak. In a skillet heat the shortening and brown the meat.

Transfer the meat to a 7 1/2 x 12-inch baking dish. Blend the remaining flour mixture into the pan drippings. Stir in the remaining ingredients, and stir constantly until thick and bubbly. Pour the mixture over the meat, and cover the dish. Bake in a 350° oven for about 1 hour and 20 minutes, or until the meat is tender.

Serves 6.

Pat Rasmussen—Cokato, Minnesota

Barney's Salt and Pepper Steak

1 1/2 pounds sirloin steak
1/2 cup oil
1 onion, chopped
1 green pepper, chopped
1/2 teaspoon salt

1/4 teaspoon pepper
3 tablespoons all-purpose flour
1 cup water
3 tablespoons soy sauce
Cooked rice

Cut the steak into very thin slices. In a skillet with a lid heat the oil and add the steak slices. Cook uncovered until browned. Pour out some of the oil and add the remaining ingredients except the rice. Cover and cook for 30 to 35 minutes, until the juice has thickened. Serve over rice.

Serves 4 to 6.

Harriet Patterson—Greensboro, North Carolina

At Morelli's:
ANDY: The special's awful good.
GOOBER: Yeah, the special's good!
GLORIA: What is it?
GOOBER: A dollar seventy-five.

85

Diner Pounded Steak

À la Juanita.

Pound a round steak with the edge of a saucer. In a shallow bowl combine 1 cup flour, 1 teaspoon salt, and 1/4 teaspoon pepper (as much as needed in these proportions). Cut the steak into pieces and roll in the flour. Fry the steak pieces in hot oil or melted shortening until brown.

Use the oil to make gravy.

Figure on about 1/4 to 1/2 pound of steak for each person, according to their appetites.

Betty Burroughs—Lebanon, Tennessee

Best Beef Tenderloin

1 3- to 4-pound beef tenderloin	3 tablespoons soy sauce
1/2 cup chopped onion	2 teaspoons dry mustard
1 1/2 tablespoons butter or margarine, melted	1/8 teaspoon salt
1 cup dry sherry	1/8 teaspoon pepper

Trim the excess fat from the tenderloin and place in a large shallow baking pan. Bake in a 400° oven for 10 minutes.

In a skillet or saucepan sauté the onion in butter until tender. Add the remaining ingredients and bring to a boil. Pour the mixture over the tenderloin. Reduce the oven temperature to 325° and bake for 35 minutes, or until a meat thermometer reaches 150° to 170°. Baste often with the drippings.

Serve the tenderloin with the remaining drippings.

Serves 8 to 10.

Ben Weaver Beef Burgundy

Great eating's in store with this one.

1/2 pound diced beef suet (or 1/4 cup shortening)	1 cup dry red wine
3 pounds lean beef chuck, cubed	1/2 pound fresh mushrooms, sliced (or 1 4-ounce can)
3 tablespoons all-purpose flour	12 small white pearl onions (or 1 large onion, chopped)
1 1/2 teaspoons salt	Hot fluffy mashed potatoes
1/2 teaspoon pepper	Crisp green salad
1/2 teaspoon dried thyme	Hot bread
1 10 1/2-ounce can condensed beef broth, undiluted	

About 4 hours before dinner, heat the suet in a large skillet until crisp, and then remove it. In the hot fat, brown the meat. Stir in the flour, salt, pepper, and thyme, scraping the bottom of the skillet well. Turn into a 2-quart casserole. Pour the beef broth and wine over the meat. Cover and bake in a 325° oven for 2 hours.

Add the mushrooms and onions. If the mixture seems dry, add more beef broth and wine in equal portions. Continue baking for 1 hour and 30 minutes, until the meat is tender. Remove from the oven and skim the fat from the gravy.

Serve with mashed potatoes, crisp green salad, and hot bread.

Serves 6.

Sue Concelman—Houston, Texas

Beef Stroganoff Barney

Real food.

1 pound very lean flank steak	1 cup beef broth
1 tablespoon butter	3 tablespoons sherry (optional)
1 large onion, finely chopped	Salt and pepper
1 clove garlic, very finely chopped	1 cup sour cream (or low-fat yogurt)
2 cups thinly sliced mushrooms	2 cups cooked noodles, freshly cooked and
1 tablespoon cornstarch	still hot
1/4 teaspoon dill weed	1 cup finely chopped parsley

Slice the steak into very thin strips, about 1/2 by 2 1/2 inches. In a large skillet heat the butter. Sauté the onions and garlic, stirring frequently. Add the steak and mushrooms, and cook until the meat is browned on all sides. In a small bowl mix the cornstarch, dill weed, broth, and sherry until smooth. Stir into the steak mixture and simmer for 5 minutes. Add salt and pepper to taste. Stir in the sour cream and serve over the hot noodles. Sprinkle parsley over all.

Variation: 2 cups of cooked hot rice could be substituted for the noodles, but the Russians wouldn't like it.

Serves 4.

Gene Wyatt—Nashville, Tennessee

Suppertime at the Taylors':

ANDY: Roast beef and no company? Well, boy, folks are really gonna say we're getting uppity. Having roast beef, and it ain't even the weekend.

Hungry as a bear

Sheriff's Shepherd Pie

A tempting dish for Mayberry's crooks.

1 1/2 pounds ground beef
Onion (I use dry minced onion)
Favorite vegetable (green beans, peas, etc.)

Buttered mashed potatoes
Grated cheese (optional)

In a skillet brown the beef and onion. Place the mixture in the bottom of a casserole dish. Add the vegetable next, and cover with mashed potatoes. Top with grated cheese if desired. Bake in a 350° oven until warmed through and the top is browned.

Serves 4 to 6.

Marti Downs—Sparta, Tennessee

Charlotte's Kraut Casserole

1 16-ounce can sauerkraut
1 16-ounce can corned beef
3/4 cup biscuit mix
3/4 cup milk

1/2 cup mayonnaise
3 eggs
11/4-ounce package Swiss cheese, sliced

In a 9 x 13-inch baking dish spread the sauerkraut and top with the corned beef. Combine the biscuit mix, milk, mayonnaise, and eggs, and pour over the kraut and corned beef. Arrange the cheese slices over the batter. Bake in a 400° oven for 30 to 35 minutes.
Serves 8 to 10.

Charlotte Womack—Browns Summit, North Carolina

County Cork Cornish Pasties

2 large baking potatoes
1 tablespoon bacon grease
1/2 cup chopped onion
1 to 11/2 cups water
1 12-ounce tin corned beef (not the hash)

Salt and plenty of pepper
Pie crust pastry
1 egg
1/3 cup milk

Peel the potatoes and slice into 1/4-inch slices. In a saucepan heat the bacon grease and slightly sauté the onion. Add the sliced potatoes and cover with water. Bring to a boil. Reduce the heat, cover, and simmer until the potatoes are fork tender, about 15 minutes. Drain any remaining water, and add the corned beef. Stir well. Slightly mash some of the potatoes as you stir. Add the salt and pepper. Let the mixture cool to room temperature.

Roll the pie crust into individual 8- to 9-inch circles. Place 1 cup of the meat and potato mixture on half of each circle, fold over, and press the edges to seal. Beat together the egg and milk, and brush over the pasties. Place on a baking sheet. Bake in a 350° oven for about 45 to 50 minutes or until light brown. These are good served at room temperature.
Makes enough filling for about 4 pasties.

Susan Ryman—Houston, Texas

BARNEY: (To Aunt Bee) You keep feeding us like that and the next thing you know they'll be calling me Porky. (Pauses to notice disbelief on her and Andy's faces.) It's possible.

Fun Girls Wonton

2 cups sifted all-purpose flour
1 teaspoon salt
2/3 cup lukewarm water
Cornstarch
1/4 pound ground beef, pork, or chicken
1 green onion, minced
1/4 teaspoon salt

1/8 teaspoon freshly ground black pepper
1/2 teaspoon soy sauce
1/2 teaspoon dry sherry
1 tablespoon broth or water
1 egg, beaten
Oil for deep frying

Sift the flour and salt into a bowl and make a well in the center. Pour the water into the well. With a wooden spoon stir until the dough forms a ball. Turn onto a floured surface and knead until stiff. Cover with a damp cloth and let the dough stand for 30 minutes. Sprinkle the board with cornstarch and roll the dough into a long strip 6 inches wide and less than 1/8 inch thick. Cut into 3-inch squares.

In a bowl mix together the meat, onion, salt, pepper, soy sauce, sherry, and broth. Place 1 teaspoon of the mixture in the middle of each square. Moisten the edges of the squares with beaten egg and press the opposite corners together to form a triangle. Fry in hot oil until golden brown.

Makes about 36 wontons.

Andy's Roast Beef Burritos

Here's the beef.

Oil
1 clove garlic, minced
1 small onion, chopped
4 cups leftover roast beef, shredded
4 to 5 fresh tomatoes, chopped
1 6-ounce can chopped green chili peppers

1/2 teaspoon cumin
1 8-ounce can taco sauce
1 package flour tortillas
1 8-ounce can enchilada sauce
1 cup grated cheddar cheese

In a skillet heat a small amount of oil and sauté the garlic and onion until tender. Add the beef, tomatoes, chili peppers, cumin, and taco sauce. Simmer for at least 1 hour. If desired, the dish may be thickened by adding cornstarch or a mixture of 1/4 cup flour and 1 cup cold water. Heat the tortillas. Spoon the meat onto the tortillas and roll up.

Heat the enchilada sauce and add the cheese. Stir constantly until the cheese is melted. Watch closely to prevent the cheese from sticking to the pan. Spoon the red sauce onto the burritos and enjoy!

Serves 6.

Mary Jane Allen—Birmingham, Alabama

Ragout Raleigh

A capital success.

Bacon
1 pound round steak
Salt and pepper
3 carrots, sliced paper thin

1 medium onion, sliced
3 or 4 potatoes, very thinly sliced
Parsley flakes

In a very heavy skillet arrange half strips of bacon over the bottom. Cut the round steak in strips and cover the bacon with the strips. Add salt and pepper. Cover the meat with the sliced carrots and onions, top with the potatoes, and add salt, pepper, and parsley flakes. Cover and cook over very low heat for 2 hours to 2 hours and 30 minutes, until done. Do not lift the lid unless it is cooking too fast and needs a little water. It can be cooked longer if necessary—just make sure it is on low heat.

Serves 4.

Grandma Concelman—Houston, Texas

Andy and Barney working late at the courthouse:

BARNEY: You know, we ain't had supper yet, Ange. It's almost 7 o'clock. You know me and my low-sugar blood content. I'll be getting a headache in a minute, and I won't be any good to anybody.

ANDY: Hey, I got an idea. [Won't] take too long to go out. Why don't you run over to the Diner and bring back a couple of sandwiches.

BARNEY: That's a good idea.

ANDY: Yeah.

BARNEY: You know what I'm gonna get? Two chili-sized burgers with chopped onions, catsup, piccalilli, and mustard, side of French fries, slab of rhubarb pie, and chocolate malt. How does that hit you?

ANDY: That'll lay on your chest.

BARNEY: You work it off, man. You work it off.

ANDY: Oh, Barn, I don't believe . . .

BARNEY: Will you leave it to Mr. Fix-It?

ANDY: O.K.

BARNEY: Where's the car—front or back?

ANDY: Back. Now don't dawdle. I don't want to eat that food cold.

BARNEY: Are you kidding? The Diner guarantees their food to stay hot—hours after you've eaten it.

Andrew Paul Lawson's Lasagna

Some think it's rich, but it really isn't.

1 pound ground beef
1 onion, chopped
Garlic, minced
1 15-ounce can tomato sauce
1 6-ounce can tomato paste
Salt and pepper to taste
Half a 16-ounce package lasagna noodles

1 egg, beaten
1 1/2 cups large-curd cream-style cottage
   cheese
1 teaspoon salt
1 8-ounce package sliced mozzarella
   cheese
1/3 cup grated Parmesan cheese

In a saucepan brown the ground beef, onion, and garlic. Add the tomato sauce, tomato paste, salt, and pepper. Simmer for 1 hour. Cook the noodles in boiling salted water until tender, and drain. Combine the egg, cottage cheese, and 1 teaspoon of salt. Mix well.

Grease a 3-quart casserole dish. Layer half of the noodles, half of the meat sauce, half of the cottage cheese, half of the mozzarella, and half of the Parmesan. Repeat the layers. Bake in a 375° oven for 30 minutes. Let the lasagna stand for 15 minutes before serving.

Serves 6.

Goober's Secret Spaghetti Sauce

1 large onion
1 medium green pepper (optional)
1 tablespoon butter
1 1/4 pounds ground beef
1 6-ounce can tomato paste
1 4 1/2-ounce jar sliced mushrooms
2 14 1/2-ounce cans stewed tomatoes
1 15-ounce can tomato sauce

1 teaspoon thyme
1 teaspoon oregano
1 bay leaf
Salt and pepper to taste
1 package Italian spaghetti sauce mix
1 teaspoon garlic salt
1/2 cup water
Cooked pasta, tossed with butter

Chop the onion and green pepper. In a large skillet heat the butter and sauté the onion and green pepper until tender. Remove from the skillet. Add the ground beef to the skillet and cook until browned. In a large saucepan combine the sautéed onion and pepper, browned ground beef, and remaining ingredients except the pasta. Simmer over low heat for about 1 hour.

Serve the sauce over the buttered pasta. Do not combine the pasta with the sauce before serving. The sauce can be frozen for use later.

Serves 6.

Tim White—Blountville, Tennessee

Goober describes his spaghetti sauce in Spaghetti Dinners—Round 1 of a scheduled three-round bout:

GOOBER: It's all in the special sauce—my very own *secret* sauce.

ANDY: Oh, a secret, huh? Did you make it up out of your own head?

GOOBER: It's a family hand-me-down with a secret ingredient, so it won't do you any good to ask what it is.

ANDY: O.K., I won't.

GOOBER: Oregano.

ANDY: Huh?

GOOBER: You mix it with something called oregano.

ANDY: Oh, oregano. That's the secret ingredient?

GOOBER: Yeah.

Mother Sprague's Family Spaghetti Sauce

2 6-ounce cans tomato paste
Water
1 teaspoon garlic salt
1 teaspoon onion salt
1 teaspoon celery salt

1 teaspoon parsley
Oregano to taste
1 pound ground beef
Cooked spaghetti
Grated cheese

In a saucepan combine the tomato paste, 4 tomato paste cans of water, the garlic salt, onion salt, celery salt, parsley, and oregano. Bring to a boil, reduce the heat, and simmer for 2 to 3 hours.

In a large skillet brown the ground beef. Add the sauce, and simmer for 30 minutes. Serve over cooked spaghetti, and sprinkle with cheese.

Serves 4 to 6.

Ellen Young-Fagrelius—Phoenix, Arizona

Briscoe Darling discovers Aunt Bee's cooking:

BRISCOE: Well, Miss Bee, you sure ain't lost your touch with a skillet. Tell me something. What was that thing you had laying there twixt the taters and the black-eyed peas?

AUNT BEE: The steak?

BRISCOE: Mouthwaterin'. Gotta learn what kinda animal you chomp that off of.

Howard Sprague

Every mother would be proud to have a son like Howard. He always buttons up his coat before going out in the cold, and he brushes his teeth for fifteen minutes before retiring at night. Of course, Mrs. Sprague is not pleased when Howard decides to join the local lodge, a haven for guzzling root beer.

But any son who gets plenty of vitamin C can always redeem himself. And eventually, after his mother marries and moves away, the likable county clerk follows his rainbow and discovers new horizons of fishing, bowling, and dating. As he is quick to find, "My pot of gold is right here in Mayberry."

Spaghetti Dinners—Round 2:

ANDY: That certainly is delicious spaghetti, Mrs. Sprague—especially that sauce of yours.

MRS. SPRAGUE: Oh, thank you, Andrew. It's something of a secret recipe—handed down through five generations of the Sprague family.

ANDY: Oh, a secret? Well, whatever it is in there, it certainly is tantalizing.

MRS. SPRAGUE: I really shouldn't tell you, Andrew, but it's a Greek spice called . . . oregano.

ANDY: Oh-oh. Well, who in the world would think of putting oregano in a sauce?

HOWARD: That's what makes it a *secret* recipe, Andy.

ANDY: Oh, I guess it would, wouldn't it?

Uncle Edward's Secret Spaghetti Sauce

1 tablespoon oil
1 onion, chopped
1 pound ground beef
1/2 clove garlic, minced
4 tablespoons chopped parsley
1/2 teaspoon pepper
1/2 cup Parmesan cheese

2 15-ounce cans tomato sauce
2 6-ounce cans tomato paste
1 tablespoon wine vinegar
1/2 teaspoon oregano
1/2 teaspoon crushed basil
1 teaspoon salt
Cooked spaghetti

In a skillet heat the oil and brown the onion. Add the ground beef, garlic, 2 tablespoons of parsley, 1/4 teaspoon of pepper, and 1/4 cup of Parmesan cheese. Cook until the beef is browned, and transfer to a dish.

In the same skillet combine the tomato sauce, tomato paste, vinegar, oregano, basil, salt, 2 tablespoons of chopped parsley, 1/4 teaspoon of pepper, and 1/4 cup of Parmesan cheese. Simmer for 15 minutes. Add the ground beef mixture and simmer for 30 minutes.

Serve with cooked spaghetti.

Serves 6.

Doug Sprecher—Greensboro, North Carolina

MENU: Goober's hamburger order: Hamburger with catsup, mustard, hot sauce, pickles and onions, French fries on the side, and an orange drink.

Spaghetti Dinners—Round 3 and Andy's down for the count:

ANDY: Well, what do you know—spaghetti!

HELEN: Well, I can't take credit for the entire meal. Uncle Edward supervised the sauce.

UNCLE EDWARD: Yeah, I got the recipe from a famous Italian chef in New York City.

ANDY: Is that right?

UNCLE EDWARD: Yeah, it took me all evening to wheedle it out of him.

ANDY: Bet it did.

UNCLE EDWARD: You're not kidding. But I used my wits. Actually, it all centers around one secret ingredient . . .

ANDY: Oregano.

UNCLE EDWARD: (Disappointed) Yeah. How do you know?

ANDY: (Embarrassed) I guessed.

Courthouse Crock Pot Spaghetti Sauce

Mayor Stoner stumbled across this one day.

1 1/2 pounds ground chuck, browned
1 1/2 cups chopped onion
2 cloves garlic
1 14 1/2-ounce can tomatoes
2 6-ounce cans tomato paste

1 1/2 teaspoons salt
2 teaspoons dried oregano
1/4 teaspoon thyme
1 bay leaf

In a crock pot combine all of the ingredients. Stir thoroughly and cook on low for 10 to 12 hours, or on high for 4 to 5 hours.

Serves 6.

Robin and Tommy Ford—Northport, Alabama

More Power to Ya Meatballs

Briscoe guarantees them to make you "strong as an ox and almost as bright."

1 1/2 to 2 pounds ground beef
1 medium onion, grated or minced
20 Ritz crackers, crushed
1/4 teaspoon black pepper
1/4 teaspoon garlic salt
1/2 teaspoon dry mustard
2 large eggs, beaten

1 1/2 cups bottled barbecue sauce
3/4 cup tomato paste
1 teaspoon liquid smoke
1/3 cup catsup
1/3 cup brown sugar
1/2 cup water or as needed

In a large bowl combine the ground beef, onion, crushed crackers, pepper, garlic salt, dry mustard, and eggs. Squish the mixture together by hand until well mixed, and form into walnut-sized balls. Place them on a flat wire rack in a roasting pan or a large cake pan. Bake the meatballs in a 350° oven for 15 minutes, turn, and bake for 15 minutes more.

In a saucepan combine the remaining ingredients. Cook over medium low heat for 30 minutes. Add the meatballs and simmer for several hours. This may also be done in a crock pot.

Makes about 60 meatballs.

Linda and Jack Densmore—Denton, Maryland

Flora's Meat Loaf Malherbe

A favorite down at the Diner.

1 pound ground beef
Dash celery seed
1/2 cup chopped onion
1/3 cup milk
1/4 cup bread crumbs

1 egg, beaten
1 tablespoon Worcestershire sauce
3 tablespoons brown sugar
3/4 cup catsup

In a large bowl combine the ground beef, celery seed, onion, milk, bread crumbs, egg, and Worcestershire sauce. Shape into a ball and place in a baking pan. Combine the brown sugar and catsup, and pour over the top of the meat loaf. Bake in a 350° oven for 45 minutes.

Serves 4.

Bobbie Carson—Nashville, Tennessee

The Spaghetti Dinners saga continues:
 OPIE: You mean you're going to leave all that food on your plate, Paw?
ANDY: Well, uhh . . .
 OPIE: What about what you told me this morning?
ANDY: What was that?
 OPIE: You know, about all the people in the world not having enough to eat and how it's almost a crime for us not to finish everything on our plate.
ANDY: Well, Opie, there are extenuating circumstances.
 OPIE: I even told our scoutmaster what you said, and he said that if more people felt that way, it would be a better world.
ANDY: He's a fine man.
 OPIE: If this food weren't here, it might be in India, so we should eat it and not let it go to waste.

> GOOBER: (Talking about Flora) Once her hand brushed up against mine when she put down a plate of succotash. I think she done it on purpose.

Dipsy Doodle Hamburger Noodle Casserole

Oil
1 medium onion, finely chopped
1 pound ground beef

1 16-ounce box macaroni
1 10½-ounce can cheddar cheese soup

In a skillet heat a small amount of oil and brown the onions. Add the ground beef and brown. Drain off the fat.

Cook the macaroni according to the package directions and drain. Add to the beef mixture, along with the soup. Heat through. Transfer to a casserole dish to serve, if desired.
Serves 4.

M. S. Smith—Greensboro, North Carolina

Andy and Barney sitting on the porch after Sunday dinner:
BARNEY: Man, we really packed it away, didn't we?
  ANDY: Yeah, boy.
BARNEY: (Pats tummy) Fortunately, none of mine goes to fat. All goes to muscle.
  ANDY: Does, huh?
BARNEY: It's a mark of us Fifes. Everything we eat goes to muscle. (Pats tummy) See there?
  ANDY: I see.
BARNEY: My mother was the same way. She could eat and eat and eat . . .
  ANDY: Never went to fat . . .
BARNEY: (Nods) Know where it went?
  ANDY: Muscle?
BARNEY: (Nods) It was a mark of us Fifes . . .

Aunt Bee's Fried Chicken

1 frying chicken	All-purpose flour
2 eggs, beaten	Shortening
Salt to taste	

Wash and cut up the chicken. Dip the pieces in the beaten egg, season with salt, and roll in the flour. Put a right smart amount of shortening in a frying pan and melt it. When it's good and hot, turn it down a little and fry the chicken slowly. Turn the chicken pieces over 3 to 4 times and cook slowly for about 15 to 20 minutes. After it gets brown, put a lid over the chicken and simmer for 20 minutes.

Serves 4 to 6.

Lois Rogers—Readyville, Tennessee

ANDY: M-mm. I tell you, Aunt Bee. That sure was good.

AUNT BEE: Well, I'm glad you liked it.

ANDY: We're going to have to give you a title or something. Miss Fried Chicken of Mayberry.

AUNT BEE: Oh, stop it. Now, help me with the dishes.

Orange Chicken Helen

4 chicken breasts, boned and skinned	Orange sections
Butter	Currants
Salt	Raisins
Orange juice	Diced walnuts (optional)
Tabasco sauce	Rice pilaf

Flatten the chicken breasts slightly. In a skillet heat a small amount of butter and cook the chicken breasts for about 5 minutes on each side. Salt lightly. Add orange juice to cover, and simmer for a few minutes. Add Tabasco sauce to taste, orange sections, currants, raisins, and walnuts as desired. Cover and simmer for about 25 minutes, until the chicken is tender. Check, and add more orange juice if needed.

Serve with rice pilaf.

Serves 4.

Aneta Corsaut—cast member

Clara's Oven Fried Chicken

2 to 3 eggs
1 frying chicken, cut up
Salt and paprika

All-purpose flour
Shortening

Break the eggs over the chicken, add salt and paprika, and coat the chicken pieces well, mixing by hand. Roll the chicken in flour.

In a baking pan or skillet melt the shortening, heating until very hot. Place the chicken in the very hot shortening. Bake in a 400° oven until the chicken is done and golden brown. Be sure to turn the chicken over during baking.

Serves 4 to 6.

Ruby Rogers—Woodbury, Tennessee

Opie is sent to his room for not eating the first supper Aunt Bee makes for Andy and him:

ANDY: Say, Opie, you know a funny thing happened? We come back to clear the table, and you know that plate of yours and all the food on it had disappeared.

OPIE: Really?

ANDY: Yeah. And I just . . . (Looks behind Opie) Well, I'll be dogged. There's your plate. Right there.

OPIE: Oh, yeah.

ANDY: Well, how in the world do you reckon it got all the way up here to your room— and licked clean to boot?

OPIE: I think I got an explanation, Paw.

ANDY: You do?

OPIE: Yeah, I brought it up for my bird.

ANDY: For Dickie there? Well, do you mean to tell me that he eats fried chicken and biscuits and honey?

OPIE: He loves it.

ANDY: He does?

OPIE: See how he cleaned his plate?

ANDY: You sure you ain't got a buzzard in that cage?

OPIE: Pretty sure.

ANDY: Dickie, if I was you, I wouldn't be doing any flying tonight, because them biscuits can lay awful heavy. . . . Say, Opie, do you reckon that Dickie would like to have a nice big piece of watermelon for dessert?

OPIE: Yeah!

Write-On Chicken Marsala

¹/₂ cup all-purpose flour	¹/₂ teaspoon dried basil
1 large frying chicken, cut into pieces	¹/₂ teaspoon oregano
4 tablespoons olive oil	2 cups dry Marsala wine
Salt and freshly ground pepper	1 10-ounce jar red currant jelly
¹/₂ teaspoon rosemary	2 cups sour cream, at room temperature

Place the flour in a bag, and shake the chicken pieces in the flour. In a skillet heat the oil and brown the chicken. Season with salt, pepper, rosemary, basil, and oregano. Pour 1 cup of the Marsala over the chicken, and simmer uncovered for 10 minutes. Transfer the chicken and sauce to a casserole dish and add the remaining Marsala. Bake in a 350° oven for 45 minutes or until tender.

In a separate pan melt the jelly and blend in the sour cream. Just before serving, remove the chicken from the casserole and blend the jelly mixture into the sauce in the casserole. Serve the sauce in a serving bowl separately.

This is very good served with noodles.

Serves 6.

Harvey Bullock—writer

Karate Cashew Chicken

You'll flip for this.

2 egg whites, slightly beaten	¹/₂ cup cashew pieces
¹/₂ cup cornstarch	3 tablespoons soy sauce
1¹/₂ pounds uncooked chicken breast, cut into bite-size pieces	1 cup chicken stock
6 tablespoons oil	1 tablespoon cornstarch
2 slices fresh ginger root, minced	1 6-ounce package frozen Chinese pea pods, broken in half
1 tablespoon white wine	1 16-ounce can bean sprouts, drained
2 teaspoons sugar	

Place the egg whites in a shallow bowl. Place ¹/₂ cup of cornstarch in a shallow dish. Dip the chicken pieces in the egg whites and coat with the cornstarch. In a skillet heat the oil. Add the ginger root and chicken. Stir fry until the chicken changes color, and add the wine, sugar, cashews, and soy sauce. Combine the chicken stock and 1 tablespoon of cornstarch. Lower the heat and pour the chicken stock mixture into the chicken mixture. Add the pea pods and bean sprouts. Cover and simmer for 10 minutes. Serve with rice.

Serves 4.

Mrs. Foster's Chicken à la King

2 tablespoons butter
1 teaspoon minced onion
1/3 cup chopped green pepper
1/2 cup all-purpose flour
3 cups chicken stock
3 cups diced cooked chicken
1 cup chopped mushrooms, cooked

1/2 teaspoon salt
1/4 teaspoon pepper
2 egg yolks
3/4 cup milk (more or less for desired thickness)
1/3 cup chopped red pimento

In a skillet melt the butter and sauté the onion and green pepper until slightly brown. Remove vegetables from the skillet. Add the flour, blending well. Add the stock and cook until thickened. Add the chicken, mushrooms, sautéed onion and green pepper, and seasonings, and heat through. In a small bowl beat the egg yolks and add the milk. Stir the milk mixture into the chicken mixture, and stir until blended. Add the pimento. Remove from the heat and serve.

Serves 8.

Charlie Lee's Chicken Chow Mein

A Canton Palace specialty.

Butter
1 cup finely chopped celery
1 medium onion, chopped
2 10 1/2-ounce cans cream of mushroom soup

1 4-ounce can sliced mushrooms
1/2 cup cashews, unsalted
2 whole or 4 individual chicken breasts, cooked and cut up
1 12-ounce can chow mein noodles

In a skillet melt a small amount of butter and cook the celery and onion until tender and the onion is transparent. Add the mushroom soup, drained mushrooms, cashews, and chicken pieces. Mix well. The casserole may be frozen at this point if desired. Turn the mixture into a large casserole dish. Bake uncovered in a 350° oven for 45 minutes. Remove from the oven and add three-fourths of the chow mein noodles. Mix well and bake for 10 minutes. Sprinkle the remaining noodles over the top and bake for 5 more minutes.

Serves 4 to 6.

Gail Baddeley—Toronto, Ontario

Fred Goss's Chicken with Dried Beef

They'll clean their plates with this no-fuss dish.

3/4 pound dried chipped beef

6 strips lean bacon

6 chicken breasts, boned

1 10 1/2-ounce can cream of mushroom soup

In the bottom of a shallow casserole dish arrange the dried beef. Wrap a strip of bacon around each chicken breast, and arrange over the beef. Spread the undiluted soup over the chicken, and cover with aluminum foil. Bake in a 300° oven for 2 hours. Increase the heat to 350° and bake for 20 to 30 minutes, basting several times.

Note: No seasoning is required. The bacon and beef will season the chicken enough. But you may want to add a little black pepper or a little sherry to the sauce for the last few bastings before serving. For beauty's sake, some mushrooms may be added if desired.

Serves 6.

Margaret Hooper—Houston, Texas

Waiting for the gold shipment

Gold Shipment Broiled Chicken

Shhh! It's top secret.

3 tablespoons butter
1 3-pound chicken, cut into pieces
1 1/2 teaspoons salt

1/4 cup honey
1/4 cup prepared mustard
1 tablespoon lemon juice

Line a 9 x 13-inch pan with foil. Melt the butter in the pan. Place the chicken skin-side down in the pan and sprinkle with 1/2 teaspoon of salt. Blend the remaining salt, honey, mustard, and lemon juice. Brush half of the honey mixture on the chicken. Bake in a 350° oven for 30 minutes. Turn the chicken and brush with the remaining honey mixture. Bake for 30 minutes more, or until the chicken is tender.
Serves 4.

Tara Concelman—Houston, Texas

A Capella Chicken Enchilada

Right on key even without accompaniment.

1 medium onion, chopped
2 to 3 tablespoons butter
1 10 1/2-ounce can cream of chicken soup
1 10 1/2-ounce can cream of mushroom soup
1 cup chicken broth

1 4-ounce can green chilies, chopped
1 chicken (or 8 breasts), boiled and boned
1 package corn tortillas
1 pound longhorn cheese, grated

In a skillet brown the onion in butter. Add the soups, broth, and chilies. Add the chicken and mix well. In a large baking dish, layer some of the corn tortillas, part of the chicken mixture, and some of the grated cheese. Repeat the layers until the dish is filled, ending with cheese. Let the dish stand for several hours before baking. Bake in a 350° oven for 1 hour.
Serves 10.

Hope Blueher—Alameda, New Mexico

Fortune cookie futures:
GOOBER: You are going to meet a tall, handsome stranger.
HELEN: Spend the day with good friends.
HOWARD: Be considerate of others. It will return manyfold.
ANDY: Try to avoid temptation in the coming week.
AUNT BEE: Beware of business ventures. They can prove costly.

Mrs. MacGruder's cousin

Mrs. MacGruder's Chicken and Dressing

Clean your plate and you can have some more.

1 whole chicken
3 quarts water
2 teaspoons salt
2 quarts cornbread, crumbled
6 slices white bread crumbs (or 6 biscuits), crumbled

1 tablespoon rubbed sage
1/4 teaspoon black pepper
1 onion, chopped
1/2 cup chopped celery
4 eggs

In a large stock pot boil the chicken in the water with the salt for 1 hour, until tender. Reserve the chicken stock.

In a large bowl combine the cornbread, white bread, sage, black pepper, onion, and celery. Add the stock from the chicken until the mixture is the consistency of cornbread batter. Don't leave it too dry. Add more broth or water if necessary. In a small bowl beat the eggs, and add to the dressing mixture. Pour the mixture into a large baking pan. Bake in a 350° oven for 1 hour.

Serve with the cooked chicken.

Mary Pearl Harrison—Houston, Texas

The daily traumas of life in Mayberry:

ANDY: Something botherin' you?

BARNEY: Aw, I don't know—just wondering where we're going to eat lunch.

ANDY: What about the Diner?

BARNEY: I checked the special on the way in. Chicken wings, rice, and mixed vegetables.

ANDY: That don't sound bad.

BARNEY: You know what she does: She gives you two wings—and usually from a chicken that's done a *lot* of flyin'. What you wind up paying for is the rice and mixed vegetables. That's what it boils down to, you might as well face it.

ANDY: Well, we don't have to have the special.

BARNEY: I guess we don't have to.

ANDY: Diner then?

BARNEY: O.K.

Checkpoint Chickie Pan Pie

If you take one bite, you'll take five.

1 3¹/₂- to 4-pound roasting chicken or hen
Salt and pepper to taste

1 batch biscuit dough
Butter, if broth is not rich enough

In a saucepan boil the chicken until tender in 3 to 4 cups of water with salt and pepper. Remove the chicken from the broth, and reserve 2¹/₂ cups of broth. Skin and bone the chicken, and cut into large chunks. Thicken the reserved broth.

Grease a 9-inch square baking dish. Roll a portion of the dough as thin as for pie crust, and cut into strips. Line the bottom of the dish with the strips. Roll the remaining dough fairly thin, cut with a medium biscuit cutter, prick with fork tines, and brush the tops with melted butter or buttermilk.

Arrange the chicken over the strips in the baking dish, season to taste, and cover completely with the thickened broth. Cover with the prepared thin biscuits, placing them close enough to touch. This will require about 10 to 14 biscuits, depending on the size. Bake in a 375° to 400° oven until the biscuits are cooked through and browned on the top and the pie is bubbly. Additional broth may be added during baking if needed.

Serves 6 to 8.

Eudora Garrison—Charlotte, North Carolina

Diner Special Chicken and Rice Casserole

3 tablespoons corn oil
1½ cups chopped green pepper
¾ cup sliced onion
¼ cup cornstarch
2 cups chicken stock

3 tablespoons soy sauce
2 cups shredded cooked chicken
3 tomatoes, chopped
Hot cooked rice

In a skillet heat the oil and add the peppers and onions. Cover and cook over low heat until tender but not brown.

Blend the cornstarch with a little bit of chicken stock. Add the remaining stock and the soy sauce. Gently stir the shredded chicken and the stock mixture into the vegetables. Cook, stirring constantly, until the sauce is clear and thickened. Add the tomatoes and heat through. Serve over hot rice.

Serves 4 to 6.

Tara Concelman—Houston, Texas

Jim Lindsay and Andy in accord

Jim Lindsay's Chicken and Dumplings

They're the best.

1 chicken

1 recipe dumpling dough (see Raleigh Rolled Dumplings on p. 68)

Boil the chicken in salted water for a couple of hours. Take out the chicken, leaving the broth for the dumplings. Roll out the dough until it's paper-thin. If it's too thick, they won't be any good. Slice the dough in strips and drop them into the boiling broth. Don't you dare stir them, or you'll have mush. It takes about 10 minutes for them to cook.

Serves 4 to 6.

Lois Rogers—Readyville, Tennessee

Howard Sprague's Spinach-Stuffed Pork Roast

Just like Mother used to make.

1 3- to 5-pound pork roast, double loin, rolled and tied
1/4 cup chopped fresh mushrooms
1/4 cup chopped onion
1/4 cup chopped red pepper
1 tablespoon oil
Half a 10-ounce package frozen chopped spinach, thawed

1 cup soft bread crumbs
1/4 teaspoon salt
1/4 teaspoon pepper
1/8 teaspoon sage
1/8 teaspoon garlic powder
Kumquats (optional)
Cranberries (optional)
Holly sprigs (optional)

Untie the roast and set aside. In a skillet cook the mushrooms, onion, and red pepper in hot oil until tender. Stir in the spinach, bread crumbs, salt, pepper, sage, and garlic powder. Spread the stuffing over one loin to within 1 inch of the edge. Top with the remaining loin. Tie securely with string.

Place the roast on a rack in an open roasting pan. Insert a meat thermometer in the thickest part of the roast, not touching fat. Bake uncovered in a 325° oven for 2 to 3 hours, allowing 30 to 35 minutes per pound, or until the meat thermometer registers 165°. Remove from the oven, and let stand for 10 to 15 minutes. The temperature will rise about 5 degrees to reach the recommended internal temperature of 170°, and juices will set.

Garnish with kumquats, cranberries, and holly sprigs, if desired.

Serves 6 to 8.

Sue Concelman—Houston, Texas

Civil servants

Foley's Ribs

Make no bones about it—they're the best in town.

4 pounds pork loin country-style ribs
1 medium onion, chopped
1/2 cup light molasses
1/2 cup catsup
2 teaspoons finely shredded orange peel
1/3 cup orange juice
2 tablespoons oil
1 tablespoon vinegar

1 tablespoon bottled steak sauce
1/2 teaspoon prepared mustard
1/2 teaspoon Worcestershire sauce
1/4 teaspoon garlic powder
1/4 teaspoon salt
1/4 teaspoon pepper
1/4 teaspoon bottled hot pepper sauce
1/8 teaspoon ground cloves

In a large saucepan add enough water to the ribs to cover. Bring the mixture to a boil and reduce the heat. Cover and simmer for 45 to 60 minutes, until tender. Remove from the heat and thoroughly drain.

In a small saucepan combine the remaining ingredients. Bring the mixture to a boil, and reduce the heat. Boil gently, uncovered, for 15 to 20 minutes, until the sauce is reduced to 1 1/2 cups. Stir once or twice.

Grill the ribs over slow coals for about 45 minutes. Turn every 15 minutes and brush with the sauce until the ribs are well coated. Arrange the ribs on a serving platter and pass the remaining sauce.

Serves 6.

Yes, Juanita, There Is a Snappy Lunch!

The Snappy Lunch, a landmark in Andy Griffith's hometown of Mount Airy, North Carolina, since 1923, is one of a handful of actual Mount Airy businesses mentioned on *The Andy Griffith Show* that are still around today.

One of the big reasons for the thriving Snappy Lunch business is its mouthwatering pork chop sandwich. Folks flock from miles around just to get a whiff of one.

Snappy Lunch owner Charles Dowell is the creator of the sandwich and other Snappy Lunch specialties, such as the distinctive breaded hamburger, that customers go out of their way to enjoy.

Dowell, a humble but engaging man, started out sweeping floors at the Snappy Lunch around 1943 when he was fourteen. After a short time in the insurance business, he became a partner in the Snappy Lunch in 1951. Coming from a family (including fourteen brothers and sisters) raised in the grocery and restaurant business, Dowell was well prepared for his career and has been at home standing over the Snappy grill ever since.

You'll find a loyal following of happy patrons at the Snappy Lunch for breakfast and lunch (closed for supper). Many are regulars who drop by for lunch about as often as Andy and Barney might have done at the Diner in Mayberry.

"It used to be that there were only about five places you could eat in Mount Airy," Dowell recalls. "They were all right here on Main Street. Everything was centered right in the middle of town. There were few automobiles, so folks walked to everything.

"On Saturday nights, folks would be packed in here waiting for the picture show to start across the street at the Grand. In those days, most folks stood to eat because it was too crowded to sit."

The Snappy Lunch is still packing 'em in, though a while back Dowell did add some tables and lowered the countertop to give customers more places to sit and eat. He also added a bigger grill, but it stayed right in Snappy's front window, where Dowell can still survey Main Street and wave to passersby while flipping pork chops.

Though modest almost to a fault, Dowell is rightfully proud of the food served at the Snappy Lunch. He is obviously flattered that so many customers enjoy the food served at his café. The Snappy Lunch has been an important part of Charles Dowell's life for most of his life and most of this century.

Dowell rarely takes vacations, and when he does, the Snappy Lunch closes while he's gone. "It's really hard to get me off that grill," he chuckles. He adds seriously, "I don't know what I'd do without this place. It's really all I've ever known."

It's lucky for Dowell that lots of other people do take vacations and go sightseeing. These days, he says, there are sometimes as many tourists dropping by the Snappy Lunch as there are regulars. "A day doesn't go by that somebody doesn't come in wondering whether this is the real Snappy Lunch mentioned on *The Andy Griffith Show* and some of Andy Griffith's records."

If the delicious food and Dowell's neighborly demeanor don't completely satisfy their appetite for the flavor of Mayberry, then the Snappy Lunch also has plenty of photos of

Andy Griffith and other Mayberry memorabilia on display to please any fan of the show.

Though the Snappy Lunch opens before dawn and closes around two in the afternoon (also closed all day on Sunday), Dowell and his wife, Mary, will often stay long after closing to answer questions from curious visitors.

"It's just hard to turn folks down," Dowell says. "Oftentimes, they've come from a long way just to get a glimpse of where Andy Griffith once walked. *Andy Griffith* fans truly are a different breed. They're the nicest people in the world. Their excitement about visiting Mount Airy gets me excited, too. I really enjoy meeting the people that come by.

"And it's really amazing the number of people who *do* come by," Dowell adds. "They genuinely love that old show and come here looking for some reminder or souvenir of Mayberry."

And if there has ever been someone who exhibits the genuine friendliness of Mayberry, it's Charles Dowell. No visitor goes away disappointed after meeting him and feeling his appreciation for all that *The Andy Griffith Show* means to him.

"I keep waiting for the popularity of the show to wear off and keep thinking that there won't be as many tourists coming by. But the last few years I believe there have been more people than ever. I'm just grateful for all that Andy Griffith has meant to this town."

But make no mistake: It's Snappy's tasty fare—not its novelty—that keeps folks coming back again.

A Snappy breakfast has all the mainstays: bacon, country ham, and sausage, grits and gravy, homemade biscuits, orange juice, and coffee. But it's lunch that sets Snappy apart.

"We make our own chili every day," says Dowell with pride. "We make our own slaw every day, and we make our own batter for the pork chops every day. We still use a steam bun warmer. The pork chop sandwich is not easy to make. You have to stand right over it and cook it just right. People tell me there's nowhere else to get one like it, and I believe they're right."

And the same goes for the breaded hamburger—made each day from freshly ground beef. "Some folks don't like the breaded hamburger at first because it is different. But once they've had it and kind of acquire a taste for it, they'll go out of their way to get it. I'd say 99 out of 100 people that come in will want the breaded hamburger over a regular hamburger. It's another thing you can't get anywhere else that I know of."

On top of all that appeal, Snappy's prices are practically right out of Mayberry during the '60s. Indeed, the Snappy Lunch may be part of a disappearing era, but it thrives by providing things that never go out of style: friendliness, fast service, value, and, of course, delicious food. Pass it on!

Update: This story was written for the original 1991 edition of this cookbook. Charles Dowell died in 2012. His wife, Mary, continues to oversee the Snappy Lunch. She shares ownership with daughter, Jamie, whose husband, Seth Dowell-Young, now usually mans the legendary grill behind the window looking onto Mount Airy's Main Street.

Snappy Lunch Pork Chop Sandwich

This recipe for Snappy Lunch's famous pork chop sandwich has been a closely watched secret for decades—never before being published until now. We're grateful to Charles Dowell for sharing it with Aunt Bee. Preparation of this sandwich is not easy to master, and you really can't beat having one prepared at the Snappy Lunch. But here's how they do it if you want to try it for yourself!

Remove the bone from the pork chop and trim the fat. Tenderize the chop by pounding. Make sure that the chop is not too juicy. If you wash your pork chops, make sure you dry off the excess water.

The secret is in the batter, which is also the tricky part. Start with 2 cups of plain flour (do not use self-rising flour). Add 2 tablespoons of sugar, 2 whole eggs, and salt to taste. The proportions of ingredients are the same for larger batches of batter.

Gradually add sweet milk and beat the mixture until it is completely smooth—not lumpy but also not watery. The consistency is very important. When you dip a spoon in the batter, the batter should run freely off the spoon without being watery. (If the batter runs off the spoon too freely, it'll run off the pork chop the same way.)

Get the grease in your skillet or griddle hot but not too hot. That is: hot enough to cook the meat but not so hot that the batter scorches.

Dip the pork chop generously in the batter and then place it in the skillet. Don't rush it. Impatience will lead to brown batter and raw meat. Turn the chops occasionally.

When the meat is cooked, the chop is ready to eat. At Snappy Lunch the sandwiches are served on a steamed bun and topped with homemade chili, homemade slaw, onions, tomato, and mustard. Enjoy.

Note: The same batter used for the pork chops makes outstanding onion rings. However, you might want to make the batter just a fraction thinner by adding more milk.

Snappy Lunch Potato Cakes

The Snappy Lunch hasn't served potato cakes in years, but folks still ask about them decades later. Here's the recipe for this old Snappy favorite:

Prepare mashed potatoes (instant is fine) with plenty of butter (or margarine) and season them just as if you were going to serve them ready to eat on the table. Add 3/4 cup of plain flour (not self-rising) for every cup of mashed potatoes. Add one whole egg per cup of potatoes. Mix all the ingredients together. Gradually add a little water or milk for moistening. The mixture should be able to fall easily off a spoon, but be careful not to make the mixture actually runny.

Dip out teaspoons of mixture and toss them into a moderately greased skillet. Fry until golden brown and crispy on the outside. (The thinner the cake, the better.) Some folks like to mix in onions with their potatoes as well. More power to you!

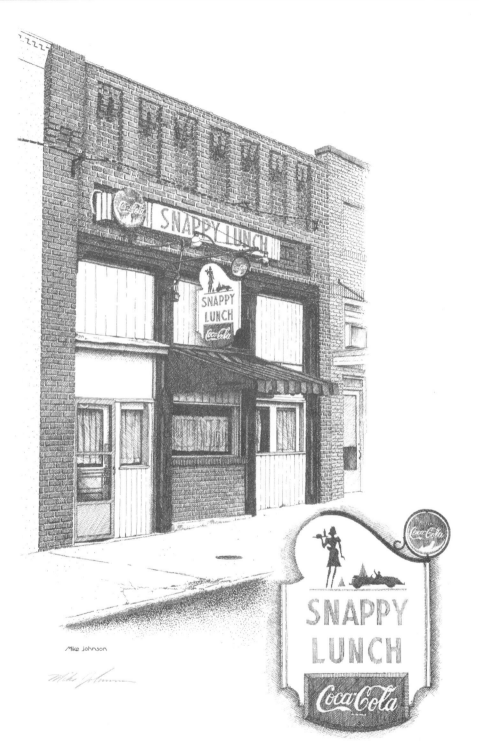

Mike Johnson

Pipe Down Pork Chop Casserole

4 or 5 potatoes
4 or 5 pork chops

1 10½-ounce can cheddar cheese soup
1 10½-ounce can French onion soup

Slice the potatoes into a 9 x 11-inch casserole dish. Arrange the pork chops over the potatoes. Combine the soups and pour over the pork chops and potatoes. Cover with foil. Bake in a 350° oven for 1 hour.
Serves 4.

Bobbie Carson—Nashville, Tennessee

Coca-Cola Pork Chops

Bottle of pop chops.

8 pork chops
Salt and pepper to taste
1 cup catsup

1 cup Coca-Cola
Brown sugar

Place the pork chops in a baking pan. Season with salt and pepper to taste. Mix the catsup and Coca-Cola, and pour over the pork chops. Sprinkle with brown sugar. Bake uncovered in a 350° oven for 1 hour or until the pork chops are tender.
Serves 8.

Melissa Gray—Nashville, Tennessee

Mrs. Pendleton's Stuffed Pork Chops

The school board apologizes for these being so good.

6 pork chops, 1¼ to 1½ inches thick
Salt and pepper to taste
1½ cups toasted bread crumbs
½ cup chopped unpared apple
½ cup shredded sharp natural cheddar
  cheese

2 tablespoons golden raisins
2 tablespoons butter or margarine, melted
2 tablespoons orange juice
¼ teaspoon salt
⅛ teaspoon cinnamon

Have a pocket cut in each pork chop along the fat side. Salt and pepper the insides of the pockets. In a bowl toss the bread crumbs, apple, cheese, and raisins together. In a separate bowl combine the melted butter, orange juice, salt, and cinnamon, and pour the mixture over the bread crumb mixture. Mix gently. Lightly stuff the pork chops with the mixture.

Place in a shallow baking pan. Bake in a 350° oven for 1 hour and 15 minutes. Cover lightly with foil and bake for 15 minutes more.

Serves 6.

Freida Crawley—Nashville, Tennessee

Hog Winslow's Sausage Casserole

1½ pounds lean pork sausage
4 to 5 spring onions including tender portions of tops, chopped
1 medium bunch celery including leaves, chopped
1 large green pepper, chopped

Salt and pepper to taste
2 packages dry chicken noodle soup mix
4½ cups boiling water
1 cup raw brown rice
1 8-ounce can sliced water chestnuts, drained
¼ cup slivered almonds

In a large heavy skillet cook the sausage, stirring until crumbled. Remove from the fat and reserve. Pour off all but 2 to 3 tablespoons of fat. Sauté the onions, celery, and green pepper, seasoning to taste.

In a saucepan cook the chicken noodle soup in the boiling water for about 7 minutes. Add the brown rice and water chestnuts. Remove from the heat and add the sausage and sautéed vegetables. Turn the mixture into a large casserole dish. Sprinkle with almonds, and cover. Bake in a 350° oven for 1 hour and 30 minutes to 2 hours. Remove the cover for the last 30 minutes of baking.

Serves 8 to 10.

Eudora Garrison—Charlotte, North Carolina

Roger Hanover's Ham Loaf

No joke—this one's delicious.

3 tablespoons butter, melted
½ cup brown sugar
1 8-ounce can crushed pineapple
1 pound lean ground ham
2 eggs, slightly beaten

1 cup quick oats (1-minute type)
½ cup milk
¼ teaspoon pepper
¼ teaspoon ginger
1 tablespoon prepared mustard

In a 9 x 5-inch loaf pan combine the butter and brown sugar. Drain the pineapple, reserving ¼ cup of the juice. Spread the pineapple over the butter and brown sugar. Combine the reserved juice and the remaining ingredients and mix well. Press into the prepared pan. Bake in a 350° oven for 50 minutes. Invert the loaf to serve.

Serves 6.

Margaret Hooper—Houston, Texas

Grocery grab-bag

Rodney Darling's Blackened Pig

1 medium to large pig   Sauce (optional)
1 medium-size house

Run the pig into the house. Shut all of the doors. Set the house afire. Return in 3 days with oven mitts. Search and serve.

Serve with sauce if desired.
Serves the entire Darling family.

Rodney Dillard—cast member

Sweet-and-Sour Wild Pig

Chopped sooey.

1 1/2 pounds pork shoulder, cubed   1/4 cup vinegar
1/2 cup water   2 to 3 tablespoons soy sauce
1 20-ounce can pineapple chunks in heavy 1/2 teaspoon salt
　 syrup   1 small bell pepper, diced
1/4 cup brown sugar   1/4 cup diced onion
2 tablespoons cornstarch   Hot cooked rice

In a large skillet with a cover, brown the pork in a small amount of fat. Add the water, cover, and simmer for about 1 hour, until tender. Do not boil.

Drain the pineapple, reserving the syrup. Combine the brown sugar and cornstarch. Add the pineapple syrup, vinegar, soy sauce, and salt. Add to the pork. Cook and stir until the gravy thickens. Add the pineapple, bell pepper, and onion. Cook for 2 to 3 minutes. Serve over hot rice.

Serves 4 to 6.

Mrs. Fran Smith—Baytown, Texas

Ernest T.'s Possum and Sweet Taters

Sticks to your ribs.

1 1/2-pound baking potato
1 young opossum (dressed weight about 2 1/2 pounds)
4 teaspoons salt

3/4 teaspoon black pepper
1/8 teaspoon red pepper
3 tablespoons all-purpose flour
2 pounds sweet potatoes, peeled

Peel the baking potato and place it inside the possum. Place the possum in a large kettle, and cover with cold water. Boil gently, uncovered, for about 30 minutes. Pour off the broth and add fresh water. Return to a boil and cook slowly, partially covered, until tender when pierced, but not falling off the bone. Remove the possum to a roasting pan and sprinkle with salt and pepper.

Blend the flour with cold water until smooth. Combine the flour mixture with enough of the hot broth to make 2 cups of gravy. Arrange the sweet potatoes around the possum. Pour the gravy over the meat and potatoes. Cover. Bake in a 375° oven until the potatoes are nearly done, about 20 minutes. Uncover and bake, basting often, until the meat browns and the potatoes are soft, about 40 minutes.

Serve hot. This is good with turnip greens, cornbread, and baked apples.

Grace Farrar—Lebanon, Tennessee

An Ernest invitation:
ERNEST T.: I dropped by to invite you up to my cave to eat. Got some possum steaks—nice and tender. Been beatin' at them with a stick.

Roast Leg of Lamb

Andy's favorite dish.

6 cloves garlic, chopped
2 to 3 pounds potatoes, peeled and thinly
  sliced
Salt and pepper to taste
1 tablespoon fresh thyme
2 large onions, very thinly sliced

5 medium tomatoes, cored and sliced
  horizontally
2/3 cup dry white wine
1/3 cup olive oil
1 6- to 7-pound leg of lamb, trimmed of
  all fat

Rub a large 16 x 10 x 2-inch gratin dish with garlic. Layer the potatoes in the dish with salt, pepper, and a little of the thyme. Strew on a little garlic. Place the onions and tomatoes on the potatoes, and season with salt, pepper, and thyme. Add the white wine and oil.

Season the lamb with oil, salt, pepper, thyme, and garlic. Set a rack over the vegetables and place the lamb on the rack. Roast uncovered for about 1 hour and 30 minutes to 2 hours, or until the vegetables are tender and the meat registers 130° on an internal thermometer. To serve, carve the lamb into thin slices and put on a warm plate. Arrange the gratin around the lamb.

Serves 8 to 10.

Patsy Curtis—Charlotte, Tennessee

Warren's Rabbit Pie

Tastes like magic in your mouth.

2 young rabbits
1 onion, sliced
1 slice bacon, cut in strips
1 teaspoon salt

Dash pepper
All-purpose flour
Biscuit dough

Dress and wash the rabbits. Cut into serving pieces. In a large stock pot cover the rabbits with boiling water. Add the onions, bacon, salt, and pepper. Cover tightly and simmer until tender.

Remove the rabbits from the broth and place in a baking dish. Thicken the broth with flour, using 2 tablespoons for each cup of liquid. Pour the thickened broth over the rabbits. Prepare the biscuit dough and pat into a 1/4-inch-thick sheet. Place the dough over the baking dish, cutting slits to allow the steam to escape. Bake in a 450° oven for 30 minutes.

Serves 8.

Alice and Jim Schwenke—Houston, Texas

Old Man Kelsey's Barbecued Raccoon

Dress and wash the raccoon carefully so that no hair clings to the meat. Be sure the scent glands (located under the legs) have been removed. Chill thoroughly or freeze so that the fat will harden. Remove all fat and discolorations.

Place the raccoon in a large kettle and cover with cold water. Add 2 tablespoons of salt and a hot red pepper pod. Bring to a boil and simmer until the meat is tender when pierced with a fork, about 1 hour to 1 hour and 30 minutes.

Remove the meat to a roasting pan. Drizzle 1/2 cup of cider vinegar over the meat, inside and out. Sprinkle with a small amount of black or red pepper, as desired. Cover and bake with barbecue sauce for 30 minutes at 400°. Then uncover and bake until browned.

Sweet potatoes can be peeled and partially cooked in the broth, then baked with the meat. A young raccoon can be baked slowly with barbecue sauce (without parboiling) as you would pork ribs. Baste every hour and cook until the meat falls off the bone, about 4 to 6 hours.

Serves 6.

Grace Farrar—Lebanon, Tennessee

Charlene's Fish Muddle

2 pounds white fish fillets
1/3 cup melted butter
1/4 cup diced green pepper
1/2 cup diced onion
1 potato, peeled and diced
1/2 pound mushrooms, sliced
1 15-ounce can whole kernel corn

2 10½-ounce cans cream of mushroom
   soup
Milk
1/4 cup white lightning (wine)
1 teaspoon salt or to taste
1 teaspoon pepper
2 ounces chopped pimento

Cut the fish into small cubes, and set aside. In a stock pot sauté the green pepper, onions, potato, and mushrooms for 8 to 10 minutes, stirring often. In a saucepan combine the corn, soup, 2 soup cans of milk, and the wine. Heat and simmer for 5 minutes, stirring until smooth. Add slowly to the fish mixture, stirring constantly until the chowder is near boiling. Add the salt, pepper, and pimento. Hold to just below boiling for 5 minutes.

Serves 6 to 8.

Maggie Peterson Mancuso—cast member

"Everybody back on the truck."

BRISCOE: We're knowed as a family of hearty-eatin' men and beautiful, delicate women.

Mitch's Dear Darling Venison

Venison is wonderful meat, the finest product of an animal that chooses its diet all of its life—a lot more than you can say for a cow. A deer rambles around, picking a leaf here and a bud there and a lot of tender things like clover and alfalfa and soybeans and roasting ears and strawberries. By the time he finishes up on acorns, rose hips, apples, and other fall fatteners, his flesh is the ideal wild meat. No supplements, no chemicals, no fat to mention, although he stores up plenty in other places.

You take a whole deer ham and marinate it for several hours with ladles-full of white port wine, teriyaki sauce, and garlic salt. The alcohol cooks away, of course, but it leaves the fine nutty flavor that port wine is famous for, and it tenderizes the meat something wonderful. Use lots of black pepper and salt, and keep the meat wet with marinade for the best part of the day at room temperature.

The big part of cooking deer meat is suet, as deer fat is scarce and rank and causes what people call the wild taste. That isn't the wild taste of venison at all as you'll find out. Beef suet is the secret to cooking deer meat, and except for feeding birds, that's about all it's good for, and it's free. You crisscross the roast with strips of suet and cook it like beef, basting it every half hour or so. You can cook it rare, like a standing rib, or done if you like it that way, but cook it until the outside is crisp and brown and your suet has turned to cracklings. What's left of the marinade will turn the gravy into a feeding frenzy.

Now if you try that and still throw off on venison, you are probably the sort of person who wouldn't like squirrel gravy, which is equivalent to admitting you have the taste buds of a store window dummy.

Mitch Jayne—cast member

The Darlings invade the Taylors' for supper:
AUNT BEE: I was admiring your hearty appetites.
BRISCOE: I bet it does your heart good to see a real eater at work, huh?
ANDY: You all cooking for yourselves now that Charlene's married, are you?
BRISCOE: Oh, the boys there. They been takin' turns. They're just about the worst cooks they is. Just the other night they cooked up about the worst mess of grub I ever did see—hoot owl pie! Perfectly good hoot owl, just plumb wasted.

Charlene's Hoot Owl Pie

1 28-ounce can hominy, drained	$1/4$ teaspoon salt
$1/2$ pound cooked hoot owl, diced (or chicken, if desired)	Pepper to taste
	$1/4$ cup bread crumbs
1 $10^{1}/2$-ounce can cream of mushroom soup	1 tablespoon butter
4 tablespoons milk	Paprika

Butter a casserole dish. Place a layer of hominy in the bottom, then a layer of hoot owl. Continue layering until all of the hominy and hoot owl are used. In a saucepan heat the soup, milk, salt, and pepper. Pour over the casserole. Sprinkle the bread crumbs over the top, dot with butter, and dash with paprika. Bake in a 375° oven for 30 minutes.

Variation: Diced cooked lean pork or possum may be substituted for the hoot owl, if desired.

Serves 6.

Maggie Peterson Mancuso—cast member

Briscoe Darling's Hoot Owl Pie

1 good-sized cooked hoot owl, boned and chopped	1 cup sour cream
1 stalk celery, diced	1 $10^{1}/2$-ounce can cream of hoot owl soup
1 onion, chopped	Salt and pepper to taste
1 tablespoon oil	Warm tortillas
1 10-ounce package frozen broccoli, cooked and drained	$1^{1}/2$ to 2 cups hoot owl broth
	1 cup grated rat cheese

Mix the chopped owl, celery, onion, oil, cooked broccoli, sour cream, hoot owl soup, salt, and pepper together. Then you let them sit while you and the boys play "Never Beat Your Mother with a Great Big Stick." Be sure you don't play more than 6 choruses.

Roll all of this stuff into the warm tortillas and place them in a baking dish. Then pour the hoot owl broth over them. You cook all of this stuff in a 325° oven for 20 minutes or 3 choruses of "Dirty Me, Dirty Me, Oh How I Hate Myself." Make sure the onions are done. Then the last 5 minutes of cooking, place the grated rat cheese on top. Dish out the warm tortillas and hot sauce.

Now then, if the moon is in the "getgone" and the wind blows in snuffs, there ain't goin' to be no hoot owls. In that case, you get Ernest T. Bass to steal you a good-sized chicken and ya put that in instead. If you do that, while the chicken is cookin' you get the boys and play 6 choruses of "Don't Dance on the Table Charlene You Stepped in My Collard Greens."
Serves 6.

Denver Pyle—cast member

Fast-Gun Fife's Fast Flounder Fillets

There are only two kinds of cops—the quick and the dead. Here's a light dish that's packed with protein but won't stuff you to the point of slowing you down.

1 pound flounder fillets (4 to 5 small ones)
1/3 cup milk
1 tablespoon butter
2 tablespoons lemon juice
1/8 teaspoon pepper
1/4 teaspoon garlic salt
2 tablespoons dried chives

Place the fillets around the outer edge of a 9- or 10-inch glass pie plate. Pour the milk over the fillets, dot with butter, and season with the remaining ingredients. Cover with waxed paper and microwave on high for 5 minutes. Let the fillets stand covered for 5 minutes. The fillets should be moist and flake easily with a fork.
Serves 2 to 3.

Bill and LuAnne Dugan—Wynne, Arkansas

Wholly Smoked King Mackerel

A prince of a main dish.

King mackerel fillets
Lemons
Black pepper
Brown sugar

Place the fillets in a large, shallow pan. Squeeze the lemons over the fillets and sprinkle generously with pepper. Cover the fillets with brown sugar. Flip the fillets over and repeat the process. Marinate for 1 hour. If the fish has been frozen, do not marinate for more than 10 minutes, since frozen fish soaks up lemon juice.

Grill the fish on a smoker or covered grill away from direct heat. Add hickory chips if desired. Cover and smoke the fish until the fillets are firm.

Andy Andrews—Gulf Shores, Alabama

Ernest T.'s Bass

Even Ernest T. won't throw this one back.

4 skinless bass fillets
Salt and pepper to taste
4 tablespoons milk
1/4 cup all-purpose flour
1/3 cup peanut or vegetable oil

6 tablespoons unsalted butter
1 tablespoon chopped garlic
Juice of 1 lemon
4 lemon slices
3 tablespoons chopped fresh parsley

Sprinkle the fish with salt and pepper. Pour the milk into a shallow bowl. Place the flour in a shallow dish. Dip the fillets in milk, and then in the flour. Shake to remove any excess. In a large frying pan heat the oil over medium-high heat. Add the fish and cook for about 1 minute, or until golden brown on one side. Turn and cook for about 2 more minutes, or until done. This depends on the thickness of the fillets. Transfer the fish to a warm platter. Pour off all the fat from the pan and wipe it clean with paper towels.

Melt the butter over medium-high heat. Shake the pan constantly, until the butter foams and turns light brown. Add the garlic and sauté just to heat through. Sprinkle the fillets with lemon juice and pour the garlic butter over them. Garnish each fillet with a lemon slice and chopped parsley.

Serves 4.

Carp diem

Pan-Fried Flounder Floyd

What did Calvin Coolidge say about this?

¹/₂ cup oil
¹/₂ cup cornmeal
2 teaspoons salt

¹/₄ teaspoon pepper
¹/₄ teaspoon garlic powder
2 pounds flounder fillets

In a skillet heat the oil over medium heat. In a shallow dish combine the cornmeal, salt, pepper, and garlic powder. Roll the fish in the cornmeal mixture and drop in the hot oil. Fry for 3 to 5 minutes, until browned. Turn and brown on the other side.
    Serves 4 to 6.

Tara Concelman—Houston, Texas

Floyd Lawson

Mayberry's only barber, Floyd is an unusual character. His one-chair establishment is a favorite gathering place for the menfolk of Mayberry. With clippers and comb in hand, Floyd is right at home as he cuts hair and swaps yarns with the boys.

Floyd is creative in other ways. He's a songwriter ("Hail to Thee, Miss Mayberry"), actor (Mayberry Founders Day play), and musician (trombonist). He also grows prizewinning pansies.

Rafe's Red River Catfish Fry

1 2-pound can vegetable shortening
8 to 12 fresh or thawed catfish steaks or
   fillets
Salt and pepper to taste
1 pint buttermilk

1/2 large box cornbread mix
1/2 medium onion, grated
1 to 2 eggs
4 to 6 large potatoes

In a large skillet heat the shortening, starting slowly and increasing the heat until a wooden kitchen match ignites when touched to the top of the fat. Season the fish to taste. Dredge the fish pieces in buttermilk, then in cornbread mix. Place the fish in the hot fat. When golden brown on the bottom, turn and continue frying until the other side is golden. Remove from the skillet. Keep warm in the oven, set on low.

Using the remaining cornbread mix and buttermilk, make a batter and add the onion and egg. Mold the hush puppies and fry in hot fat in the same manner as the fish. Season and place in the warm oven.

Peel and cut the potatoes into fries. Fry in the hot fat, remove, and then salt and serve with the fish and hush puppies. The potatoes and hush puppies will absorb all of the odor and taste of the fish from the fat. You may strain it and pour it back into the can to be used again at your next fish fry.

Serve with a good coleslaw to remove the curse of all the fried food. As Andy would say, "Outstandin'!"

Serves 4 "fish hungry" people.

Jack Prince—cast member

Rafe sings.

Back to nature

Frank's but No Franks

This is a favorite at Myers Lake.

1/4 pound American cheese, grated
1 7-ounce can flaked tuna, drained
2 tablespoons chopped onion
1/2 cup salad dressing
3 hard-cooked eggs, chopped

2 tablespoons chopped green pepper
2 tablespoons chopped sweet pickles
2 tablespoons chopped stuffed olives
8 hot dog buns

In a large bowl combine all of the ingredients except the buns. Fill the buns with the mixture, and wrap each bun in foil. Bake in a 325° oven for 25 minutes.
    Makes 8 sandwiches.

Ellen Young-Fagrelius—Phoenix, Arizona

STREET VENDOR: Get your hot dogs while waiting for the gold truck. Here you are. Get 'em nice and hot, while you're waiting for the gold truck. Here you are. Here are these nice hot dogs.

Diner dialer

Goober's Tuna Tune-Up Casserole

Will add spark to any table.

¹/₄ pound medium noodles (2 cups)
2 medium onions, minced
2 tablespoons butter or margarine
1 20-ounce can tomatoes
¹/₄ teaspoon garlic salt

1 teaspoon salt
¹/₄ teaspoon pepper
¹/₄ cup snipped parsley
1 7-ounce can chunk-style tuna
¹/₂ pound American cheese slices

About 1 hour before dinner, cook the noodles according to the package directions, adding the minced onions. Drain. Add the butter.

In a bowl combine the tomatoes, garlic salt, salt, pepper, and parsley. In an 8-inch square baking dish place half of the noodles, half of the tuna, and half of the cheese, and pour half of the tomato mixture over the layers. Repeat the layers, ending with tomato mixture. Bake uncovered in a 350° oven for 40 minutes.

Serves 4.

Alice and Jim Schwenke—Houston, Texas

GOOBER: They say a feller works better on a full stomach.
GOOBER: If you don't get to the Diner early enough, all the good desserts are gone.

Old Sam's Recommended Salmon Loaf

Old Sam says that as long as salmon is used, and not silver carp, this recipe is a favorite at Tucker's Lake. The best salmon to use comes from Old Man Kelsey's creek, but canned salmon works just fine.

1 7³/4-ounce can salmon, drained and flaked with bones
7 soda crackers, crushed
1 egg, slightly beaten

Half of a 10³/4-ounce can cream of celery soup
1 tablespoon lemon juice
1/4 teaspoon salt
1/4 teaspoon pepper

In a large bowl combine the salmon, crackers, egg, soup, lemon juice, and seasonings. Mix well. Divide the mixture into 2 individual serving dishes or a 1-quart glass loaf dish. Cover with plastic wrap and cook in the microwave at 60% for 5 minutes. Rotate the dish and cook at 50% for 5 minutes.

Note: The remaining soup can be combined with 1 teaspoon of Worcestershire sauce, 1 tablespoon of lemon juice, and 2 tablespoons of catsup for a good salmon sauce.

Serves 2.

Jodie Dugan—Wynne, Arkansas

Sarah's Salmon Muddle

Keep this one on the line.

2 16-ounce cans pink salmon
1/2 cup chopped green onions
3 egg whites
1 cup all-purpose flour

Couple of handfuls of crushed soda crackers
Seasoned pepper to taste
1 heaping teaspoon baking soda
Oil for frying

Drain the salmon, removing the skin and bones. Reserve the liquid. In a bowl combine the salmon, onions, egg whites, flour, crushed soda crackers, and seasoned pepper. Add the baking soda to the reserved salmon liquid, stirring until it foams up and runs over on your counter. Add the liquid to the salmon mixture in the amount necessary to make the mixture gooey.

In a skillet heat the oil. Drop the salmon mixture by big globs into the hot oil and cook over medium heat until browned on each side. Eat hot or cold.

Makes a whole bunch of muddles.

Linda Stewart—Dallas, Texas

Reel fun

Miss Crump's Salmon Croquettes

1 7³/4-ounce can salmon
2 eggs, beaten
1 teaspoon salt

Corn flake crumbs (or cracker crumbs)
1 teaspoon baking powder
Oil

Drain the salmon, reserving the liquid. Flake the salmon and remove the skin and bones. In a large bowl combine the salmon, reserved liquid, eggs, salt, and corn flake crumbs to make a firm mixture. Blend in the baking powder. Shape into croquettes, and roll in additional crumbs.

In a skillet heat the oil and fry the croquettes until lightly browned.
Serves 4.

Tara Concelman—Houston, Texas

Five-Minute Corn and Shrimp Barney Supper

Especially good for bachelors like Andy and Opie, while Aunt Bee is away.

1 10¹/2-ounce can cream of mushroom soup
¹/2 cup milk
1 teaspoon paprika
1 5-ounce can broken shrimp, drained

1 12-ounce can whole kernel corn
Pepper to taste
Toast points

In a skillet combine the soup, milk, and paprika. Stir over low heat until smooth and evenly pink. Add the drained shrimp and the corn. Add pepper to taste, cover, and cook until heated through. Serve over toast points.

Serves 4.

Alice and Jim Schwenke—Houston, Texas

Crooner's Shrimp Creole

Olive oil
2 cloves garlic, minced
2 bell peppers, diced into 1-inch squares

2 12-ounce cans stewed tomatoes
2 pounds deveined cooked shrimp
Cooked white rice

In a large skillet heat the olive oil and sauté the garlic. When the garlic just begins to simmer, add the bell peppers. Add the tomatoes and simmer long enough for the flavors to blend. Add the shrimp and allow to simmer for a couple of minutes. The shrimp will toughen if overcooked. Serve over rice.

Serves 4.

Jack Prince—cast member

No Hurry Curried Shrimp

4 pounds raw shrimp, cleaned and
   deveined
1 bay leaf
Salt
Onion flakes

$1/2$ cup butter
$1/2$ cup all-purpose flour
2 $10^1/2$-ounce cans bouillon
1 6-ounce can tomato paste
1 tablespoon curry powder

In a large stock pot cook the shrimp in water to cover with the bay leaf, salt, and onion flakes for about 10 to 12 minutes. Remove the shrimp, and cook down the stock until only 1 cup remains.

In a separate saucepan melt the butter and add the flour, stirring until smooth. Add the shrimp stock gradually. Add the bouillon and tomato paste. Dissolve the curry powder in a small amount of water, and add to the sauce. Right before serving, add the shrimp and heat through over low heat.

Serves 8 to 12.

Marie Faulkner—Greensboro, North Carolina

Fried Crawdad

"You get a line and I'll get a pole, honey."

3 eggs, beaten
1 1/2 cups milk
1 teaspoon Worcestershire sauce
1 cup fish fry
1 cup all-purpose flour
1 teaspoon baking powder

1 teaspoon salt
2 tablespoons cayenne pepper
2 tablespoons garlic powder
2 pounds peeled crawfish tails
Oil

In a bowl combine the eggs, milk, and Worcestershire sauce. In a separate bowl combine the fish fry, flour, baking powder, salt, cayenne pepper, and garlic powder. Dip the crawfish in the egg mixture and coat with the dry mixture. Heat the oil and deep fry the breaded crawfish until golden.

Serves 4 to 6.

Alice and Jim Schwenke—Houston, Texas

Larrapin' Linguine with White Clam Sauce

2 tablespoons olive oil
3 tablespoons margarine
6 cloves fresh garlic, minced

5 or 6 7-ounce cans minced or chopped
  clams, broth reserved
1/2 cup Romano or Parmesan cheese

In a skillet heat the oil and margarine, and sauté the garlic. Add the clams and warm through. Add the clam broth. Simmer for about 30 minutes with the lid cocked enough to let off a little steam. Add the cheese and mix until the cheese is melted. Serve over linguine or any other flat noodles.

Serves 6.

Jack Prince—cast member

Andy's Rockefeller

They are all they're cracked up to be.

1 small onion, grated
1 cup chopped fresh or frozen spinach,
  cooked
3 teaspoons minced parsley
2 bay leaves

1/4 teaspoon salt
1/2 teaspoon celery salt
1/8 teaspoon cayenne pepper
1 teaspoon Worcestershire sauce
1 cup butter

½ cup cracker crumbs
3 tablespoons dry sherry

2 dozen medium-sized oysters
Parmesan cheese

In a large bowl combine the onion, spinach, parsley, bay leaves, salt, celery salt, cayenne pepper, and Worcestershire sauce. In a saucepan melt the butter and add the crumbs and sherry. Add the spinach mixture and stir well. Cook over very low heat for 1 to 2 hours, stirring occasionally. Place the oysters in a casserole dish or in individual oyster shells. Cover with the spinach mixture and sprinkle heavily with cheese. Crumble additional crackers over the top. Bake in a 375° oven for about 35 minutes, until bubbly and the crumbs are deep golden brown. Then bring to Andy's house and he will help you eat it! Can be served as an appetizer or dinner with green salad and Great-Grandmother Minnie's Rolls.

Serves 6.

Andy Andrews—Gulf Shores, Alabama

Lefty's Alligator Done Right

5 pounds alligator tail meat
Lemon juice
2 cups fish fry
1 cup all-purpose flour

1 teaspoon baking powder
2 teaspoons salt
2 tablespoons cayenne
Oil

Cut the alligator meat into thin pieces, removing all white, fatty tissue. In a bowl cover the meat with lemon juice and soak it for 30 minutes. In a shallow bowl combine the dry ingredients. Coat the meat with the dry mixture and deep fry until it is golden brown.

Serves 4 or more.

Alice and Jim Schwenke—Houston, Texas

ANDY: The only excuse for not eating at mealtimes is when you're sick.

Opie Taylor

Opie is one of Mayberry's most popular kids. With his dad being the sheriff and Aunt Bee being a great cook, it's no wonder. Almost anytime he pleases, Opie can take his friends on a tour of the jail or over to his house for cookies or pie.

Like most kids, Opie has a sweet tooth for candy and bubble gum, but he has a special place in his stomach for apple pie and ice cream and for peanut butter sandwiches and milk. A growing boy has to eat. When he does grow up, Opie hopes to be a dentist. However, it's doubtful that will cure his sweet tooth.

Vegetables

Asa's Asparagus

2 to 2¹/₂ pounds asparagus
Boiling water

1¹/₂ teaspoons salt
Hollister Hollandaise (see recipe on p. 218)

Cut off the tough ends of the asparagus, and scrub well. Scrape the skin and scales from the stalks. Bunch the stalks together and tie with string. Place upright in a deep saucepan and add boiling water to a depth of about 2 inches. Add salt. Bring the mixture to a boil, cover, and cook for 15 to 20 minutes. Pierce the lower part of the stalks with a fork to test tenderness. Do not overcook. Drain well. Arrange the asparagus in a serving dish and drizzle with Hollister Hollandaise.

Serves 4 to 6.

Howard's Asparagus Casserole Sprague

1 16-ounce can green asparagus spears
4 tablespoons butter
4 tablespoons all-purpose flour
Salt and pepper to taste
¹/₂ cup milk
¹/₂ teaspoon Worcestershire sauce

Dash cayenne pepper
4 hard-boiled eggs, sliced
¹/₄ pound sharp cheddar cheese, cut in chunks
¹/₂ cup blanched almond halves
Cracker or toast crumbs

Drain the asparagus and reserve the liquid. In a heavy saucepan melt the butter. Add the flour, salt, and pepper, and blend thoroughly. Gradually add ³/₄ cup of asparagus liquid and the milk, and cook until thickened and smooth, stirring constantly. The sauce should be thick, but a bit more milk or asparagus liquid may be needed. Add the Worcestershire sauce and cayenne. Remove from the heat.

Butter a medium-sized casserole dish. Layer the asparagus, eggs, cheese, and almonds. Repeat the layers until all of the ingredients are used. Spoon the sauce over all and sprinkle with crumbs. Bake in a 350° oven for about 20 minutes, until bubbly and lightly browned.

Serves 6.

Eudora Garrison—Charlotte, North Carolina

Hollister Hoppin' John

1 pound bulk pork sausage, broken into
   small chunks
4 cups water
1 large onion, roughly minced
2 cups purple hull or crowder peas

Salt
Hot sauce
Steamed rice
Cornbread

In a Dutch oven lightly brown the sausage. Drain. Do not overbrown the sausage, as that
will render all of the fat and most of the flavor. Add the water, onion, and peas. Bring
to a boil, cover, and simmer for 30 to 40 minutes. Remove the lid and simmer, stirring
occasionally, until the pot liquor thickens. Add salt and hot sauce to taste. Serve over
steamed rice with cornbread.

   Serves 4 to 6.

Jack Prince—cast member

Barney's Spanish Club Beans

¡Sí! How you like 'em.

1 pound pinto beans
1 pound ground beef, browned
1/2 pound bacon, cooked and crumbled

1 onion, chopped
Chili powder

Cook the beans according to the package directions. Add the remaining ingredients and
turn into a casserole dish. Bake in a 400° oven for 30 minutes.

   Serves 4 to 6.

Sue Concelman—Houston, Texas

Baked Goober Beanies

Yo!

2 1-pound cans pork and beans, partially
   drained
3/4 cup brown sugar

2 teaspoons dry mustard
5 slices bacon, chopped
1/2 cup catsup

Empty 1 can of beans into a 1 1/2-quart casserole dish. Combine the brown sugar and
mustard, and sprinkle half over the beans. Top with the other can of beans and sprinkle

with remaining brown sugar mixture, chopped bacon, and catsup. Bake uncovered in a 325° oven for 2½ hours.

Serves 4 to 6.

Mary Clark—Nashville, Tennessee

Town Band Baked Beans

A real winner.

1 16-ounce can baked beans	3 tablespoons catsup
3 tablespoons brown sugar	3 tablespoons molasses
3 tablespoons finely chopped celery	¼ teaspoon salt
3 tablespoons mustard	¼ teaspoon pepper
3 tablespoons chopped onion	3 tablespoons vinegar
3 tablespoons Worcestershire sauce	Dash Tabasco sauce
4 tablespoons chopped bacon	

In a casserole dish combine all of the ingredients, mixing well. Bake in a 300° oven for 3 hours or until thick.

Serves 4 to 6.

Mrs. James K. Polk—Charlotte, North Carolina

TV dinner

Moody Gypsy Beans

4 cups water	1 tablespoon black pepper
1 6-ounce can tomato paste	1 red bell pepper, chopped
3 tablespoons paprika	1 green bell pepper, chopped
2 tablespoons Tabasco sauce	1 12-ounce jar green olives
1 teaspoon salt	1 1-pound bag dried kidney beans

In a stock pot bring the water to a boil. Add the tomato paste, paprika, Tabasco, salt, black pepper, and red and green pepper. Drain the olives and add to the soup. Boil and stir for 1 minute. Add the beans. Cover with a lid and turn to medium heat. Cook for 45 minutes to 1 hour. Add another 1/2 to 1 cup of water if needed.

Serves 6.

Carlos Rodriguez—Nashville, Tennessee

Mayberry armed forces

Bert and Ben's Sweet-and-Sour Green Beans

An easy sale to any eater.

2 16-ounce cans cut green beans	2 teaspoons salt
4 strips bacon	1/2 teaspoon pepper
1 large onion, chopped	4 tablespoons sugar
2 tablespoons all-purpose flour	1/2 cup vinegar

Open the cans of green beans. Pour out the liquid from 1 of the cans, and reserve the liquid from the other can.

In a skillet fry the bacon until crisp, and reserve the drippings. Crumble the bacon. Sauté the onion in the bacon drippings. Stir in the flour, liquid from the beans, salt, pepper, sugar, and vinegar. Bring to a boil. Add the drained green beans and crumbled bacon. Heat until warmed through.

Serves 4 to 6.

Sandi Long—Charlotte, North Carolina

OPIE: I think she's the best cook in Mayberry.

Green Beans Chinese-Style

Aunt Bee planned to try this with ham loaf.

2 tablespoons butter	1/2 pound fresh mushrooms, sliced
2 tablespoons all-purpose flour	1 14-ounce can bean sprouts, drained
2 cups milk	1 medium onion, chopped and sautéed
1 teaspoon salt	2 cups medium cream sauce
1/4 teaspoon pepper	1 cup grated cheddar cheese
2 10-ounce packages frozen French-style green beans	1 3-ounce can French-fried onions, crumbled
1 cup sliced water chestnuts	

Grease a 2-quart casserole dish. In a saucepan melt the butter. Stir in the flour until smooth. Add the milk gradually, stirring constantly. Cook, stirring, until thickened. Add salt and pepper.

In the prepared dish layer half of the beans, half of the water chestnuts, half of the mushrooms, half of the bean sprouts, half of the onions, half of the cream sauce, and half of the cheese. Repeat the layers. Bake in a 400° oven for 30 minutes. Top with fried onions and bake for 10 minutes.

Serves 6.

"They's all keyed up."—Briscoe Darling

Aunt Bee and Andy, relaxing on the front porch after supper.

AUNT BEE: Did you like the white beans you had for supper?

ANDY: Uh-huh.

AUNT BEE: Well, you didn't say anything.

ANDY: Well, I ate four bowls. If that ain't a tribute to white beans, I don't know what is.

AUNT BEE: Well.

ANDY: Eatin' speaks louder than words.

AUNT BEE: You know, your education was worth every penny of it.

It was Aunt Bee's cooking that made the Darling boys speak their only words: "About to pop" and "Great beans, Aunt Bee."

Briscoe says of her white beans: "They was good."

Breeney Green Beans

Eye-opening!

3 teaspoons olive oil
3/4 cup chopped onion
2 cloves garlic, minced
2 tomatoes, peeled and chopped
1 teaspoon grated lemon rind
1/2 teaspoon salt

1/2 teaspoon Tabasco sauce
1/2 teaspoon sugar
3/4 cup light cream
2 pounds French-style green beans, fresh or frozen

In a saucepan heat the oil and sauté the onion, garlic, and tomatoes for 3 minutes, stirring constantly. Add the remaining ingredients. Bring the mixture to a boil, then reduce the heat. Cover loosely and cook just until tender.

Serves 6.

Doug's Treat White Beans

1 pound dried navy or great northern
   beans (grown on the Darling farm)
4 strips of swine (bacon)

1 teaspoon salt
2 cups chopped ham of hog

Remove all of the rotten beans, rocks, dirt, and foreign types of beans. Wash each bean individually with a toothbrush until there's not a speck of dirt left on the beans. Boil the beans once in pure water for 2 minutes. Meanwhile fry the 4 strips of swine until almost crisp. Take the beans off the heat, drain, and rinse with hot water, so as not to put the beans into shock and cause the skins to come off. Put the beans back in clean hot water on low heat. Render the grease and add the fried swine to the beans. Add 1 teaspoon of salt, or salt to taste, and the chopped ham. Cook on low heat for about 2 hours. The beans should not be overcooked as the soup will have the consistency of library paste. The broth should be fairly clear and the beans firm and not cooked to death. If you don't like white beans, try 'em. Remember, eatin' speaks louder than words. Bone Appetite.

P.S. Goes well with Hoot Owl Pie.

Serves 6 to 8.

Doug Dillard—cast member

FOOD FOR THOUGHT TEASERS

1. Will Goober eat pretzels?
   Answer: Yo!
2. What is the most important crop in Mayberry?
   Answer: Potato
3. What was Aunt Bee's winning answer on TV's *Win or Lose* game show?
   Answer: Cinnamon with custard filling
4. What is Opie's favorite kind of pie?
   Answer: Apple
5. What food does Malcolm Merriweather paint faces on?
   Answer: Eggs

Barney's Bongo Broccoli Casserole

Can't be beat.

1 large onion, chopped
$1/4$ cup margarine
2 10-ounce boxes frozen broccoli

1 $10^1/2$-ounce can cream of mushroom soup
1 roll garlic cheese, shredded
$1/4$ cup slivered almonds

In a skillet sauté the onions in margarine. Add the broccoli, cover, and cook until done, stirring occasionally. In a 2-quart casserole dish layer the broccoli mixture, soup, and cheese. Sprinkle with almonds. Bake in a 350° oven for 45 minutes to 1 hour.
    Serves 6.

Mary Clark—Nashville, Tennessee

Bile That Cabbage Down Cabbage

1 1-pound head cabbage, cored and thinly
  sliced
Boiling water
1 teaspoon salt

1 teaspoon sugar
2 tablespoons butter or margarine
$1/8$ teaspoon pepper
1 to 2 teaspoons caraway seed

In a saucepan combine the cabbage, boiling water, salt, sugar, and butter. Cover and bring to a boil again. Simmer for about 15 to 20 minutes, just until tender. Drain any remaining liquid. Add pepper and caraway, and serve.
    Serves 4 to 6.

Lori Murphy—Nashville, Tennessee

County Clerk Creamed Carrots

Nutritious and delicious.

3 to 4 carrots, thinly sliced

Medium white sauce

In a saucepan bring water to a boil and add the carrots. Cook until tender. Drain and add to the white sauce. I never liked cooked carrots, but these are delicious.
    Serves 4.

Tara Concelman—Houston, Texas

Emmett's Carrots and Peas

2 cups cooked English peas
1 cup cooked sliced carrots
Liquid reserved from cooked peas and
   carrots

1 1/2 cups medium white sauce
Pepper

In a saucepan combine all of the ingredients except the pepper and heat through. Turn the mixture into a serving dish and season with pepper.

Serves 4 to 6.

Emmett Clark

Emmett is Mayberry's No. 1 handyman. As owner of the Fix-It Shop next to the courthouse, Emmett is especially good at repairing toasters and cuckoo clocks, but he can fix just about anything.

The popular businessman's hobbies include dancing and bowling. He even sponsors a bowling team with Andy, Goober, and Howard, despite the fact that the twenty-four dollars he spends for bowling shirts exhausts his entire yearly advertising budget. But Emmett knows you can't put a price on friendship.

Sarah's Cauliflower and Cheese Bake

They'll call for more of this with impatience.

2 tablespoons reduced-calorie margarine
6 saltine crackers, crumbled
1 10-ounce package frozen cauliflower,
   cooked and drained

4 ounces Velveeta cheese, cut into 1/2-inch
   cubes

In a small skillet melt the margarine over low heat. Add the cracker crumbs and cook, stirring constantly, until the crumbs are lightly browned. Remove the skillet from the heat and set aside.

Spray a 1-quart casserole dish with nonstick cooking spray. Arrange the cauliflower in the casserole, top with cheese, and sprinkle with the crumb mixture. Cover. Bake in a 350° oven for about 20 minutes, until the cheese is melted.

Serves 2.

Freida Crawley—Nashville, Tennessee

143

Sidecar express to the Diner

Sweet Romeena Creamed Corn

Cream of the crop.

1 16-ounce can yellow corn
1 teaspoon sugar
1/2 teaspoon salt

1 teaspoon grease, lard, or margarine
All-purpose flour
Water

In a saucepan combine all of the ingredients. Cook the mixture on the stove for a while. Blend a little flour with a small amount of water, and add the mixture to the corn. Cook a little while longer.

Serves 4.

Lois Rogers—Readyville, Tennessee

Thelma Lou's Corn Custard

2 cups canned cream-style corn
3 large eggs or 4 small, well beaten
2 cups warm milk
1 teaspoon sugar

Salt and pepper to taste
Dash nutmeg
1/2 cup bread or cracker crumbs
2 tablespoons melted butter

Grease a 6-cup casserole dish. In a large bowl combine the corn, eggs, milk, sugar, salt, pepper, and nutmeg. Pour into the prepared dish. Combine the crumbs and melted butter, tossing well. Sprinkle over the corn mixture. Bake in a 300° oven for 35 to 40 minutes, or until firm.

Serves 4 to 6.

Betty Lynn—cast member

Floyd Fritters

A cut above the rest.

1³/₄ cups all-purpose flour
3 teaspoons baking powder
¹/₂ teaspoon salt
1 egg, slightly beaten

1 cup milk
1 tablespoon melted shortening
2 cups whole kernel corn
Shortening or oil for frying

Combine all of the ingredients except the corn, blending until smooth. Fold in the corn. In a large skillet heat the shortening or oil, and drop the batter by the tablespoon into the very hot fat. Fry until browned on both sides.

Serves 6.

Sue Hooper—Houston, Texas

Plain Claude's Dilled Sour Cream and Cucumber

It'll have you beamin' over every bite.

2 medium cucumbers, thinly sliced
1 teaspoon dill weed
1 teaspoon salt
¹/₄ teaspoon freshly ground black pepper
1 tablespoon sugar
2 tablespoons red wine vinegar

2 tablespoons minced parsley
2 green onions and tops, thinly sliced
1 cup sour cream
1 tomato, cut into sixths
Parsley for garnish

In a large bowl combine the cucumbers, dill weed, salt, pepper, sugar, red wine vinegar, parsley, onions, and sour cream. Cover and refrigerate for several hours.

Turn the mixture into a serving dish. Garnish with tomato wedges and parsley.

Serves 6.

Mary Engler Putney—Sacramento, California

AUNT BEE: You sit right down. My mother always said if you eat standing up, it goes right to your legs.

Frankly Baked Eggplant

1 eggplant	1 egg, beaten
Butter	Bread crumbs
1 onion, chopped	

Cut the eggplant lengthwise and scoop out the pulp with a tablespoon. In a saucepan cook the pulp until tender. In a skillet heat a small amount of butter and fry the chopped onion. In a bowl mash the cooked eggplant and add the fried onion, egg, and enough bread crumbs to thicken. Fill the empty eggplant shells with the mixture. Sprinkle bread crumbs over the top and dot with butter. Bake in a 350° oven for 25 minutes.

Serves 2.

Frank E. Myers—crew member

A-O.K. Fried Okra

Mayberry's finest. Roger and out.

Wash the okra and cut off the ends. Cut it up, salt it, and toss it in a bowl with equal parts flour and cornmeal. In a skillet heat some shortening until melted and very hot. Reduce the heat and fry the okra until it's a little brown. Turn it over and over while cooking.

Lois Rogers—Readyville, Tennessee

A lesson in table manners:
AUNT BEE: Napkins will go on the laps.
BRISCOE: I spill on my shirt, I don't spill on my pants.
AUNT BEE: Well, nice people don't spill at all.

Classic looks

Old Lady Crump's Onion Pie

2½ pounds Bermuda onions
4 tablespoons butter
1 teaspoon salt
1 cup shredded cheddar or Swiss cheese
2 tablespoons all-purpose flour
1 or 2 eggs

Pepper
Worcestershire sauce
Tabasco sauce
¾ cup sour cream
Pastry for 9-inch 2-crust pie

Peel and slice the onions. In a skillet heat the butter and sauté the sliced onions until clear and tender. Add salt. Add the cheese and heat. Remove the skillet from the heat and allow to cool.

To the onions add the flour, egg, pepper, Worcestershire sauce, and a few drops of Tabasco. Stir in the sour cream and heat through. Set aside and allow to cool slightly. Fill the pie shell with the mixture. Top with the remaining pastry. Bake in a 450° oven for 10 minutes. Reduce the heat to 300° and bake until the crust is light brown, about 30 minutes. Cool before serving.

Serves 6.

Aneta Corsaut—cast member

147

Goober Peas

Goodness, how delicious!

3 to 4 tablespoons oil
1 small onion, chopped
1 small bell pepper, chopped
2 16-ounce cans fresh-shelled black-eyed
  peas

1 14^1/$_2$-ounce can tomatoes, cut up
Salt and pepper to taste
Hot cooked rice
Cornbread

In a saucepan heat the oil and sauté the onion and bell pepper until soft and the onion is slightly brown. Add the black-eyed peas. Add the tomatoes to the mixture, and season to taste. Cook uncovered over low heat for about 30 to 40 minutes, until the flavors are well blended but the liquid is not cooked down too much.

Serve over hot white rice with cornbread.

Variation: Fry ^{1}/$_2$ to 1 pound of crumbled pork sausage with the onion before adding the other ingredients.

Serves 1 Goober or 4 ordinary eaters.

Linda Stewart—Dallas, Texas

Siler City Snow Peas

2 tablespoons butter or margarine
4 small new potatoes, quartered
1 pound fresh snow peas

1 small onion, sliced into rings
^{1}/$_2$ teaspoon salt

In a heavy skillet melt the butter. Add the potatoes and fry over medium heat until golden and crisp. Add the snow peas, onion, and salt, and fry for 5 to 7 minutes, until the peas are crisp and tender.

Serves 6.

Poke Sallet Andy

A country classic.

Remove the stems from the poke sallet. Place in a large pan and parboil the greens, letting the greens cook down. Add a little soda to make the greens cook better. Boil until the greens go down and the water looks green, about 3 minutes or longer. Drain off the water. Place the poke in a large pot and add just enough water to keep the poke from sticking. Cook for about 1 hour and 30 minutes.

In a skillet heat a small amount of grease. Add the poke and cook until you think it's almost done. Add 3 or 4 eggs and cook until the eggs are done.

Mrs. Tommie Rogers—Woodbury, Tennessee

Hash Browns Helen

2 cups shredded American or cheddar cheese
1 10¾-ounce can condensed cream of chicken soup
1 cup sour cream
½ cup finely chopped onion
½ cup finely chopped green pepper
½ cup finely chopped red pepper

¼ cup butter, melted
¼ teaspoon salt
¼ teaspoon pepper
1 32-ounce package frozen loose-pack hash brown potatoes, thawed
1 cup crushed corn flakes
1 tablespoon butter, melted

Grease a 9 x 13-inch baking dish. In a large bowl combine the cheese, soup, sour cream, onion, green and red pepper, ¼ cup of butter, salt, and pepper. Mix well. Fold in the thawed hash brown potatoes. Turn the mixture into the prepared dish. Toss together the corn flakes and 1 tablespoon of melted butter. Sprinkle over the potato mixture. Bake in a 350° oven for about 1 hour, until the casserole is golden brown and the potatoes are tender.
Serves 8 to 10.

ANDY: (About Opie) You know, it's a good thing that boy ain't a beaver. There wouldn't be a tree left in these woods.

Rodney's Potato Pancakes

6 medium potatoes
3 eggs
6 tablespoons all-purpose flour
½ onion, grated

Salt and pepper to taste
Dash garlic
Oil
Butter

Grate the potatoes, and add the eggs, flour, onion, salt, pepper, and garlic. In a skillet heat the oil and butter until hot. Shape the mixture into patties and fry in the hot oil.
Serves 6.

Rodney Dillard—cast member

Old Man Schwamp's Scalloped Potatoes

You'll never eat these alone.

2 cups thinly sliced potatoes
1/3 cup minced onion
1 tablespoon all-purpose flour
1/2 teaspoon salt

Dash pepper
1 tablespoon butter
3/4 cup scalded milk
Paprika

Grease a casserole dish. Place a layer of potatoes in the bottom of the casserole dish. Sprinkle with some onion. Sprinkle some flour, salt, and pepper over the layers. Dot with butter. Repeat the layers until all of the potatoes, onion, flour, salt, pepper, and butter are used, ending with butter. Pour milk over all, and sprinkle with paprika. Bake covered in a 375° oven for 45 minutes. Uncover and bake for 15 minutes, or until tender.

Variation: Arrange 1 cup of cooked ham strips between the layers of potatoes and onion.

Serves 2.

Marti Downs—Sparta, Tennessee

> **ANDY:** Aunt Bee, those potatoes are a picture no artist could paint.
> **AUNT BEE:** Oh, flibbertigibbet.

Nip It in the Bud Spuds

3 pounds potatoes, peeled, cooked, and hot
1 8-ounce package cream cheese, softened
1/4 cup butter or margarine
1/2 cup sour cream
1/2 cup milk

2 eggs, lightly beaten
1/4 cup finely chopped onion
1 teaspoon salt
Dash pepper

In a large bowl mash the potatoes until smooth. Add the cream cheese in small pieces and the butter. Beat until well blended. Stir in the sour cream. In a separate bowl combine the milk, eggs, and onions. Stir in the potato mixture, salt, and pepper. Beat until light and fluffy. Place in a casserole and refrigerate for several hours or overnight. Bake in a 350° oven for 45 minutes, until the top is lightly browned.

Serves 8 to 12.

George Lindsey—cast member

Ordering out

Mayberry's Mexican Potato and Corn Casserole

¡Olé!

2 pounds potatoes, peeled and sliced
Salt and pepper to taste
4 ears fresh corn, cut off the cob, or 2 cups frozen cream-style corn
1 4-ounce can green chilies, chopped

2 tablespoons butter
2 cups buttermilk
2 tablespoons chopped chives
2 cups grated Monterey Jack cheese

Butter a 9 x 13-inch baking dish. Arrange half of the potato slices in the dish. Season with salt and pepper. Sprinkle with half of the corn and half of the chilies. Dot with butter. Repeat the layers. Pour the buttermilk over all. Bake in a 375° oven for 1 hour. Remove the casserole from the oven and sprinkle with chives. Top with the cheese, and return to the oven until the cheese melts.

Serves 8.

Patsy Curtis—Charlotte, Tennessee

151

New Mayor Potatoes

3 pounds small new potatoes
Boiling water
1 teaspoon salt
1/2 cup butter or margarine

3 tablespoons lemon juice
2 tablespoons finely chopped chives or
  parsley

Scrub the potatoes and peel a strip of skin from around the center of each potato, about 1/2 inch wide. Place the potatoes in a medium saucepan and add boiling water to a depth of 2 inches. Add 1/2 teaspoon of salt. Bring to a boil, cover, and boil gently for 20 minutes or until the potatoes are tender. Drain. Return to the heat for several minutes to dry out.

In a small saucepan melt the butter. Stir in the lemon juice, chives, and 1/2 teaspoon of salt. Pour the mixture over the potatoes, coating well. Turn into a serving dish.

Serves 8.

Andy tries to convince Rafe Hollister to turn himself in to Barney for moonshining:
ANDY: (To Rafe) . . . and Aunt Bee—she'll bring you some chicken and dumplings and
     sweet tater pie for supper.
RAFE: Chicken and dumplings?
ANDY: And sweet tater pie.
RAFE: I should have given myself up *years* ago.

Robert E. Lee Natural Bridge Sweet Tater Pone

*A special treat when made with sweet taters grown in the
Darlings' garden near Old Man Kelsey's woods.*

3 cups grated raw sweet taters
1 teaspoon nutmeg
1 cup sugar
3/4 cup pecans

1 cup milk
1 egg, beaten
3 tablespoons butter

Grease a 1 1/2-quart baking dish. In a mixing bowl combine the sweet taters, nutmeg, sugar, and 1/2 cup of pecans. Add the milk and egg. Pour into the prepared baking dish and sprinkle with the remaining pecans. Dot with butter. Bake in a 350° oven for 45 to 60 minutes.

Serves 4 to 6.

Alice and Jim Schwenke—Houston, Texas

Mr. Schwamp's Sweet Potato Soufflé

Worth standing in line for.

3 cups mashed cooked sweet potatoes
1/2 cup orange juice
1/2 cup milk
1 teaspoon vanilla extract
1/2 cup sugar
1/2 teaspoon salt

6 tablespoons butter, melted
3/4 teaspoon cinnamon
1/2 cup brown sugar
1/3 cup all-purpose flour
1 cup chopped pecans
Marshmallows

Grease a baking dish. In a mixing bowl combine the sweet potatoes, orange juice, milk, vanilla, sugar, salt, 3 tablespoons of melted butter, and cinnamon. Beat until fluffy, and pour into the prepared baking dish. Melt the remaining butter and add the brown sugar, flour, and pecans. Sprinkle the mixture over the potatoes. Bake in a 350° oven for 35 minutes. Top with marshmallows and bake until browned.

Serves 6.

Nancy Clark—Greensboro, North Carolina

Raleigh's Budding Executive Sweet Tater Casserole

Top notch.

3 cups mashed cooked sweet potatoes
1 cup sugar
2 eggs
1 teaspoon vanilla extract
1/3 cup milk

1/2 cup margarine
1 cup brown sugar
1/3 cup all-purpose flour
1/3 cup margarine
1 cup pecans

In a mixing bowl combine the sweet potatoes, sugar, eggs, vanilla, milk, and 1/2 cup margarine. Beat until smooth. Turn the mixture into a casserole dish. In a bowl combine the brown sugar, flour, and 1/3 cup margarine. Crumble the mixture over the potato mixture and sprinkle with pecans. Bake in a 350° oven for 30 minutes.

Serves 6.

Brad Thompson—Manvel, Texas

MENU: Businessman's Special at the drugstore: Egg salad sandwich, lettuce, a hollowed-out tomato, coffee (black), and a little yellow cookie.

Sarah's Succotash

Your party line will be abuzz with this one.

1 16-ounce can lima beans, drained
1 12-ounce can whole kernel corn, drained
2 tablespoons butter or margarine

1/2 cup light cream
Salt and pepper

In a saucepan combine the lima beans, corn, butter, and cream. Heat through, and add salt and pepper to taste.
  Serves 6.

Alice and Jim Schwenke—Houston, Texas

Opie's Turnip-Your-Nose Greens

2 to 2 1/2 pounds turnip greens
Salt pork strip, 1/2 x 3 inches

Salt
Water

Pick over the leaves of the greens and remove any spotted parts or discolored leaves and stems. Wash the leaves carefully and thoroughly, until they are free of sand and soil. The turnip greens will have edible white roots. Trim the stem top and root part from each, and wash thoroughly. Slice and cut into quarters, and cook with the leaves. Place all in a large saucepan and add a little water, salt to taste, and the salt pork. Bring to a boil, reduce the heat, and simmer just until tender, 20 to 30 minutes. Remove from the heat, drain, and serve immediately.
  Greens are delicious served with pork chops, sweet potatoes, and cornbread.
  Serves 4.

Ellie's Confetti Vegetables

1 cup mashed cooked carrots
1 cup frozen chopped broccoli, thawed
1 10-ounce package frozen whole kernel
  corn, thawed
1 cup milk
1 cup cracker crumbs

1/2 cup shredded sharp cheddar cheese
1/4 cup minced onion
1/3 cup melted butter
Salt and black pepper to taste
1/8 teaspoon cayenne pepper
4 eggs

Butter a round 2-quart glass baking dish. In a large mixing bowl combine the carrots, broccoli, corn, milk, cracker crumbs, cheese, onion, and butter. Season with salt, pepper, and cayenne.

"No thanks, Pa."

In a separate bowl beat the eggs until frothy. Blend lightly into the carrot mixture. Pour the mixture into the prepared dish. Bake in a 350° oven for 40 to 45 minutes or until a knife inserted near the center comes out clean.

Serve hot or at room temperature. This reheats very well.

Serves 6 to 8.

Elinor Donahue—cast member

Cousin Virgil's Veg-All Casserole

Don't worry, Virg got this one right.

2 16-ounce cans Veg-All, drained
1 10½-ounce can cream of celery soup
1 medium onion, chopped
½ cup mayonnaise

1 8-ounce can sliced water chestnuts, drained
1 stack crackers
½ cup butter, melted

Spray a 9 x 13-inch glass baking dish with cooking spray. Combine all of the ingredients except the crackers and butter, and pour into the prepared dish. Crush the crackers and toss with the melted butter. Sprinkle the crumbs over the vegetables. Bake in a 300° oven for 30 minutes.

Serves 8.

Mrs. Frank Brower—Asheboro, North Carolina

Squad Car Squash

An automatic hit.

1 8-ounce package Pepperidge Farm
  cornbread dressing mix
1/4 cup butter, melted
1 pound yellow squash, sliced
1 pound zucchini, sliced
1 large onion, chopped
1 green pepper, chopped

2 ribs celery, chopped
Salt and pepper to taste
1 8-ounce can sliced water chestnuts,
  drained
1 10³/4-ounce can cream of chicken soup
1 8-ounce carton sour cream

Butter a large casserole dish. Combine the dressing mix and butter, and press half of the mixture into the prepared dish. In a saucepan of boiling water, place the squash, zucchini, onion, green pepper, and celery. Boil for 5 to 10 minutes. Drain well. Add the seasonings and water chestnuts, and turn the mixture into the casserole dish, over the dressing mix. Combine the soup and sour cream, and spread over the vegetables. Top with the remaining dressing mix. Bake in a 350° oven for 25 to 30 minutes.
  Serves 6 to 8.

Margaret Hooper—Houston, Texas

Paradise Rice

4 cups rice, cooked
1 pound bacon, cooked and crumbled,
  drippings reserved
6 eggs, scrambled hard and finely chopped

1/2 cup soy sauce
Green onions, chopped
1 7-ounce can chunk white chicken

In a saucepan combine the rice and 1/2 cup of bacon drippings. Add the remaining ingredients and heat through.
  Serves 8.

Tina Muncy—Clarksville, Arkansas

Sheriff's Rice

1/8 teaspoon saffron, crumbled
2 tablespoons oil
2 tablespoons butter or margarine

1 1/2 cups raw long-grain white rice
1 1/2 teaspoons salt
3 cups water

In a small bowl combine the saffron and 1 tablespoon of hot water. Set aside. In a medium saucepan heat the oil and butter. Add the rice and salt. Cook, stirring occasionally, for 5 minutes. Add the saffron mixture and 3 cups of water, and bring to a boil. Reduce the heat, cover, and simmer for 15 to 20 minutes, or until the liquid is absorbed.

Serves 8.

Houdini Zucchini

There's no escape from this great-tasting dish.

1 large onion, chopped
Butter or margarine
4 large zucchini, peeled and thinly sliced

8 medium yellow squash, peeled and thinly sliced
Salt and pepper
1 8-ounce bag shredded cheddar cheese

In a large pot sauté the onion in butter. Add the zucchini and squash in layers, seasoning with salt and pepper between each layer. Cover and cook just until tender. Sprinkle the cheese over the top, cover, and cook until the cheese melts.

Serves 6 to 8.

Sandi Long—Charlotte, North Carolina

Murrillos Red Beans and Rice

Perfect whether you're a gypsy passing through Mayberry or not.

1/2 pound Polish sausage (as fat-free as possible)
1 small onion, chopped
1 large bell pepper, cored, seeded, and diced
2 ribs celery, chopped
1 clove garlic, minced (optional)

1 16-ounce can kidney beans (undrained)
1 14 1/2-ounce can tomatoes
1 cup cooked rice
1/4 cup red wine (optional)
1/2 teaspoon crushed rosemary
1/2 teaspoon thyme
Salt, pepper, and Tabasco to taste

Spray a large saucepan or Dutch oven with cooking spray and sauté the sausage, onion, bell pepper, celery, and garlic. Add the remainder of the ingredients and simmer for about 20 minutes.

Serves 4.

David Allen—Birmingham, Alabama

Thelma Lou

When it comes to sweets, Thelma Lou takes the cake. Whether it's making brownies (with Opie's help) or enjoying ice cream or a pan of cashew fudge with Barney, Thelma Lou is right at home. Together, Thelma Lou and Barney make perfect sweethearts.

Their dates are usually a real treat—dutch, that is. For a change of pace, the lovebirds also enjoy spending romantic evenings at the duck pond. Ducks or no ducks, for Barney, Thelma Lou will always be "the cat's."

Cakes, Pies, and Desserts

Hope for More Chocolate Cake

Goober always has seconds.

1 1/4 cups sifted all-purpose flour
1 teaspoon baking soda
6 tablespoons cocoa
1/2 cup shortening
1 cup plus 1 tablespoon sugar

2 eggs
1/2 cup buttermilk
1/2 teaspoon vanilla extract
1/2 cup boiling water

Combine the flour, baking soda, and cocoa. Sift the mixture 3 times. In a separate bowl cream the shortening. Add the sugar, and cream until light. Add the eggs one at a time, and beat for 2 minutes after each addition. Add the flour mixture alternately with the buttermilk, beating at medium speed after each addition. Add the vanilla. Add the water one-third at a time, beating well after each addition. Pour the batter into 2 ungreased 8-inch cake pans. Bake in a 350° oven for 20 to 25 minutes.

1 cup sugar
1/4 teaspoon salt
1/2 teaspoon cream of tartar

2 egg whites
3 tablespoons water
1 teaspoon vanilla extract

In the top of a double boiler over simmering water, combine the sugar, salt, cream of tartar, egg whites, and water. Beat with an electric mixer at top speed for 4 to 5 minutes. Remove from the heat and the simmering water, and beat for 1 minute. Add the vanilla, and blend. Frost the chocolate cake.
    Serves 8.

Hope Blueher—Alameda, New Mexico

ANDY: (To Opie at picnic) If you eat any more, you'll swell up so tight your freckles will
    fall off.

159

Opie's Carrot-Top Cake

Out of sight!

1 1/2 to 2 cups sugar
1 1/2 cups oil
4 eggs, beaten
2 cups self-rising flour
2 teaspoons cinnamon
1 teaspoon vanilla extract
2 to 3 cups grated carrots

1/2 cup chopped nuts
1/4 cup margarine, softened
1 8-ounce package cream cheese, softened
1 1-pound box confectioners' sugar
1 teaspoon vanilla extract
Milk, if needed

Grease and flour 3 cake pans. In a large bowl combine the sugar, oil, eggs, flour, cinnamon, 1 teaspoon of vanilla, carrots, and nuts in the order given. Pour into the prepared pans. Bake in a 300° oven for about 30 minutes.

Cream together the remaining ingredients, adding milk if necessary to make the icing spreadable. Spread on the cooled cake.

Serves 10 to 12.

Wendy Beck—Watertown, Tennessee

Miss Lucy's Coconut Cake

If you're cuckoo for coconut, you'll love it.

1 cup butter
2 cups sugar
4 eggs
3 cups all-purpose flour
3 scant teaspoons baking powder

1/2 teaspoon salt
1/2 cup buttermilk
1/2 cup water
1 teaspoon vanilla extract

Grease 3 cake pans and line with parchment paper. In a large bowl cream the butter and sugar. Add the eggs one at a time, beating well after each addition. In a separate bowl sift together the flour, baking powder, and salt. Combine the buttermilk and water, and add alternately with the dry ingredients to the creamed mixture. Add the vanilla and blend thoroughly. Turn into the prepared pans. Bake in a 375° oven for about 20 minutes. Don't overcook.

Remove from the oven and let stand in the pans for a few minutes. Turn onto a rack to cool slightly before filling and frosting.

Large fresh coconut, grated and milk
   reserved
2 cups sugar
2 generous tablespoons cornstarch

1/4 box confectioners' sugar
1/4 cup melted butter or margarine
1/2 teaspoon coconut flavoring
Hot water

Reserve 1/2 to 3/4 cup of grated coconut. Measure the coconut milk, and add milk if needed to make 1 cup. In a saucepan combine the remaining grated coconut, coconut milk, 2 cups of sugar, and cornstarch. Cook, stirring occasionally, until thickened, about 15 to 20 minutes. Cool slightly.

Thinly slice off the top of each layer of cake so that the filling will seep into the cake. Spread the filling between the layers of cake, sprinkling a bit of the reserved coconut over the filling on each layer before stacking the next layer on top.

Combine the confectioners' sugar, melted butter, and coconut flavoring. Add just enough hot water to make the frosting spreadable. Frost the sides of the cake.

Variations: Try this cake with lemon or caramel frosting.

Serves 10 to 12.

Lucy Gatlin—Charlotte, North Carolina

Otis's Dipsy Doodle Cake

1/2 cup butter
2 1/2 cups shortening
1 cup water
4 tablespoons cocoa
2 cups all-purpose flour
2 cups sugar
1 teaspoon baking soda
Chopped nuts

1/2 cup buttermilk
1 teaspoon vanilla extract
2 eggs
1/2 cup margarine
4 tablespoons cocoa
6 tablespoons milk
1 1-pound box confectioners' sugar

In a saucepan over medium-low heat, combine the butter, shortening, water, and 4 tablespoons of cocoa. In a bowl combine the flour, sugar, baking soda, and nuts. In a separate bowl combine the buttermilk, vanilla, and eggs. Add the mixture to the dry ingredients. Pour the hot mixture from the saucepan into the bowl and blend well. Pour into a cookie tray with sides. The batter is loose and spreads out. Bake in a 400° oven for 20 minutes.

In a saucepan combine 1/2 cup margarine, 4 tablespoons of cocoa, 6 tablespoons of milk, and confectioners' sugar. Spread on the cake while the cake is still warm.

This is a heavy, moist cake similar to brownies.

Serves 8.

Hal and Louise Smith—cast member

The dipsy doodler

Harriet's Caramel Nut Pound Cake

1 cup butter
1/4 cup shortening
1 1-pound box brown sugar
1 cup sugar
5 eggs
3 cups cake flour

1/2 teaspoon salt
1 teaspoon baking powder
1 cup milk
1 tablespoon vanilla extract
1 cup finely chopped black walnuts

Grease and flour a 10-inch tube pan. In a large bowl cream the butter and shortening. Add the brown sugar and sugar. Add the eggs one at a time, beating until creamy. Sift together the flour, salt, and baking powder, and add alternately with the milk and vanilla until blended well. Fold in the nuts. Pour into the prepared pan. Bake in a 325° oven for 1 hour, or until a cake tester inserted near the center comes out clean.

Serves 8.

Harriet Patterson—Greensboro, North Carolina

Old-Fashioned Pound Cake

Makes everything taste better.

1/2 cup shortening	1/2 teaspoon baking powder
1 cup butter, at room temperature	1 cup milk
3 cups sugar	2 teaspoons vanilla extract
5 eggs, at room temperature	2 teaspoons lemon extract
3 cups cake flour	

Grease and flour a tube pan. In a large bowl cream together the shortening, butter, and sugar. Add the eggs one at a time, beating after each addition. Sift the flour and baking powder together and add the mixture to the creamed mixture alternately with the milk and extracts. Bake in a 325° oven for 1 hour and 30 minutes. Let the cake cool in the pan for about 15 minutes.

   Serves 8.

Margaret Watson—Charlotte, North Carolina

Sourwood Mountain Pumpkin Coffeecake

1/2 cup butter	1 16-ounce can solid pack pumpkin
3/4 cup sugar	1 egg, slightly beaten
1 teaspoon vanilla extract	1/3 cup sugar
3 eggs	1 teaspoon pumpkin pie spice
2 cups all-purpose flour	1 cup firmly packed brown sugar
1 teaspoon baking powder	1/3 cup butter
1 teaspoon baking soda	2 teaspoons cinnamon
1 cup sour cream	1 cup chopped nuts

In a large bowl cream together 1/2 cup of butter, 3/4 cup of sugar, and vanilla. Add 3 eggs one at a time, beating well after each addition. In a separate bowl combine the flour, baking powder, and baking soda. Add the dry ingredients to the butter mixture alternately with the sour cream. Spread half of the batter into a 9 x 13-inch pan, spreading to the edges.

   Combine the pumpkin, beaten egg, 1/3 cup of sugar, and pumpkin pie spice. In a separate bowl combine the remaining ingredients. Sprinkle half of the brown sugar mixture over the batter, and spread the pumpkin mixture over the streusel. Carefully spread the remaining batter over the pumpkin mixture and sprinkle the remaining streusel over the top. Bake in a 325° oven for 50 minutes to 1 hour, or until a toothpick inserted in the center comes out clean.

   Makes 12 servings.

Darlene O'Toole—Huntersville, North Carolina

Courthouse Coffeecake

1/2 cup butter
1 cup sugar
2 eggs
1 cup sour cream
1 teaspoon baking powder
1 teaspoon baking soda

1/2 teaspoon salt
2 cups sifted all-purpose flour
1/2 teaspoon vanilla extract
3 tablespoons sugar
1 1/2 teaspoons cinnamon
3 tablespoons chopped nuts

Grease a Bundt or tube pan. In a large bowl cream the butter and sugar. Add the eggs, sour cream, baking powder, baking soda, salt, flour, and vanilla. Beat until smooth. Pour three-fourths of the batter into the prepared pan. In a small bowl combine the remaining ingredients. Sprinkle half of the mixture over the batter in the pan. Pour the remaining batter over the crumb mixture, and top with the remaining crumb mixture. Bake in a 375° oven for 35 minutes.

Serves 8.

Mary Clark—Nashville, Tennessee

BARNEY: Andy, this town is a piece of cake.

Ernest T. Bass's Nutty Fruit Cake

1 1/2 cups raisins
1 1/2 cups chopped dates
1 1/2 cups sugar
3 tablespoons lard
1 1/2 cups boiling water
2 1/2 cups all-purpose flour

1 teaspoon baking soda
2 teaspoons cinnamon
1/2 teaspoon salt
1 cup chopped nuts
1/2 cup chopped gumdrops

Line a tube pan or two 9 x 5-inch loaf pans with foil. In a saucepan combine the raisins, dates, sugar, lard, and boiling water. Simmer for about 10 minutes, and set aside to cool.

Stir in the remaining ingredients. Pour the batter into the prepared pan. Bake in a 325° oven for 1 hour or until done.

Serves 12.

Pat Rasmussen—Cokato, Minnesota

Darling sheriff

Dean Darling's Pineapple-Banana Nut Snack Cake

1 1/2 cups all-purpose flour
3/4 teaspoon baking soda
1/2 teaspoon cinnamon
1 cup sugar
1/2 teaspoon salt
3/4 cup oil

3/4 cup crushed pineapple with juice
2 eggs, beaten
1 cup diced bananas
3/4 teaspoon vanilla extract
1/2 cup chopped pecans

Grease a 9-inch square cake pan. In a large bowl sift together the flour and baking soda. Add the cinnamon, sugar, and salt. Make a well in the center of the flour mixture and add the oil, pineapple, eggs, bananas, and vanilla. Stir to blend, but do not use a mixer. Fold the pecans into the batter. Pour the batter into the prepared pan. Bake in a 350° oven for 30 minutes or until done.

Serves 9.

Dean Webb—cast member

165

Hometown Blueberry-Sausage Breakfast Cake

A square meal.

2 cups all-purpose flour
1 teaspoon baking powder
1/2 teaspoon baking soda
1/2 cup margarine or butter
3/4 cup sugar
1/4 cup packed brown sugar
2 eggs
1 cup sour cream

1 pound pork sausage, crumbled, cooked,
   and well drained
1 cup blueberries
1/2 cup chopped pecans
1/2 cup sugar
2 tablespoons cornstarch
1/2 cup water
2 cups fresh or frozen blueberries
1/2 teaspoon lemon juice

In a medium bowl stir together the flour, baking powder, and baking soda, and set aside. In a separate bowl beat the margarine with an electric mixer on medium speed until fluffy. Add 3/4 cup of sugar and the brown sugar, and beat until combined. Add the eggs one at a time, beating for 1 minute after each addition. Add the flour mixture alternately with the sour cream to the egg mixture, beating after each addition just until combined. Fold in the sausage and 1 cup of blueberries. Pour the batter into an ungreased 9 x 13-inch pan. Spread the batter evenly in the pan. Sprinkle the pecans evenly over the batter. At this point, you may cover and refrigerate the unbaked cake overnight.

Bake in a 350° oven for 35 to 40 minutes, or until a toothpick inserted in the center comes out clean. Cool on a wire rack.

In a medium saucepan combine 1/2 cup of sugar, the cornstarch, water, and 2 cups of blueberries. Cook, stirring frequently, for 2 minutes. Add the lemon juice, stirring to blend. Serve over the warm cake. Refrigerate any leftover cake and sauce.

Serves 15.

Blanche Cox—Florissant, Missouri

Andy's Chocolate-Filled Angel Food Cake

For devil-may-care appetites.

6 tablespoons cocoa
6 tablespoons sugar
1/8 teaspoon salt
1 1/2 pints whipping cream

1 large angel food cake
1 cup blanched almonds, slivered and
   toasted

Combine the cocoa, sugar, salt, and cream. Chill for 1 hour. Whip the chilled mixture.
Cut a 1-inch layer from the top of the angel food cake. Cut out the middle of the

cake, leaving walls and bottom about 1 inch thick. Fill the cavity with one-third of the cream mixture and one-third of the almonds. Replace the top of the cake. Frost with the remaining cream mixture and sprinkle the remaining almonds over the top and sides. Chill for 2 to 3 hours before serving.

Serves 6.

John Faulkner—Greensboro, North Carolina

Teacher's pets

Golden Rule Gingerbread

Serve unto others.

1²/₃ cups all-purpose flour
1¹/₄ teaspoons baking soda
1¹/₂ teaspoons ginger
³/₄ teaspoon cinnamon
³/₄ teaspoon salt
1 egg, lightly beaten

¹/₂ cup sugar
¹/₂ cup molasses
¹/₂ cup boiling water
¹/₂ cup oil
²/₃ cup confectioners' sugar
3 tablespoons lemon juice

Grease and flour a 9-inch square baking pan. In a bowl sift together the flour, baking soda, ginger, cinnamon, and salt. Add the egg, sugar, and molasses. Mix well. Pour the boiling water and oil over the mixture, and stir until smooth. Pour the batter into the prepared pan. Bake in a 350° oven for 35 to 40 minutes, or until the top springs back when touched and the edges have pulled away from the sides of the pan.

   Combine the confectioners' sugar and lemon juice, and pour over the hot gingerbread. Cool in the pan on a wire rack.

   Serves 12.

Best for Last Strawberry Shortcake

¹/₂ cup milk
¹/₃ cup sugar
1 tablespoon cornstarch
¹/₈ teaspoon salt
2 egg yolks, beaten
¹/₄ teaspoon finely shredded lemon peel

2 tablespoons lemon juice
1 tablespoon butter or margarine
1 teaspoon vanilla extract
1 quart strawberries, sliced
2 tablespoons sugar

In a saucepan combine the milk, ¹/₃ cup of sugar, cornstarch, and salt. Cook, stirring constantly, until thickened and bubbly. Cook and stir for 2 minutes more. In a small bowl stir about ¹/₂ cup of the hot mixture into the egg yolks. Return the egg yolk mixture to the pan and bring to a gentle boil. Cook and stir for 2 minutes more. Remove from the heat and stir in the lemon peel, lemon juice, butter, and vanilla. Cover with plastic wrap and chill. Sprinkle the berries with the sugar and set aside.

2 cups all-purpose flour

2 tablespoons sugar

1 tablespoon baking powder

3/4 teaspoon finely shredded lemon peel

1/2 teaspoon salt

1/2 cup butter or margarine

1 egg, beaten

2/3 cup light cream or milk

1/2 cup whipping cream

Butter or margarine, softened

Grease an 8-inch round baking pan. In a large bowl combine the flour, sugar, baking powder, lemon peel, and salt. Cut in 1/2 cup of butter until the mixture resembles coarse crumbs. Make a well in the center. In a small bowl combine the egg and light cream. Add all at once to the dry ingredients and stir just until the dough clings together. Spread into the prepared pan, building up the sides a little. Bake in a 450° oven for 15 to 18 minutes, or until done. Cool for 10 minutes.

Beat the whipping cream until soft peaks form. Fold into the chilled lemon sauce. Remove the shortcake from the pan and cool on a wire rack for 5 minutes. Split the cake into 2 layers and spread the bottom half with butter. Spoon half of the berries and half of the sauce over the butter. Replace the top layer. Top with the remaining berries and drizzle with the remaining sauce. Serve warm.

Serves 8.

Boysinger's Baker's Icing

It takes the cake.

1 1/2 cups milk

2 tablespoons cornstarch

1/2 cup shortening

1/2 cup butter

1 cup sugar

Dash salt

1 teaspoon vanilla extract

In a saucepan combine the milk and cornstarch. Cook until thick, and set aside to cool. In a bowl cream the shortening, butter, and sugar with an electric mixer for about 10 minutes. Add the creamed mixture to the milk mixture. Add the salt and vanilla. Beat together with the mixer until creamy like whipped cream.

This takes a little while to make, but it is great. It's one icing that doesn't melt into the cake. You can put layers together with 1/2 inch of icing in between and the icing will stay put.

Enough icing to frost a 3-layer cake.

Sue Concelman—Houston, Texas

169

Salt-and-pepper deputy with sugar

Thelma Lou's Very Chocolate Cheesecake

12 ounces chocolate wafers, crushed
3/4 cup unsalted butter, melted
32 ounces cream cheese, at room
  temperature
1 teaspoon vanilla extract

1 cup sugar
8 ounces semisweet chocolate, melted
3 large eggs
1 cup sour cream

Combine the crushed wafers and melted butter, and press into a 9-inch springform pan. It helps to use a drinking glass to press the mixture. Set the crust aside, as you do not need to bake it.

Cream the cream cheese until smooth. Add the vanilla and sugar, and beat well. Add the chocolate and beat until blended. Add the eggs one at a time, scraping the bowl and beating after each addition. Add the sour cream and beat until smooth. Pour the filling mixture over the crust, and smooth the top. Bake in a 375° oven for 1 hour. Turn the oven off and let the cake stand for several hours until completely cool or overnight. Leave in the pan, and refrigerate until cold.

1/8 cup unsalted butter, melted
3 ounces semisweet chocolate, melted
1 tablespoon water

1/2 teaspoon vanilla extract
1/3 cup confectioners' sugar
Strawberries for garnish

In the top of a double boiler over simmering water, melt the butter and chocolate. Add the water and vanilla extract, and stir until blended. Add the sugar and whisk until smooth. Pour over the cooled cheesecake, and refrigerate. Garnish with strawberries.

Serves 8.

Robert Shockley and Lynne Prettyman—Salisbury, Maryland

Aunt Bee's Apple Pie

Opie's favorite.

1/2 cup butter or margarine
4 ounces cream cheese
2 cups all-purpose flour
2 1/2 cups sliced apples
1 cup sugar

1/3 cup orange juice
2 tablespoons honey
1/2 teaspoon cinnamon
1 tablespoon all-purpose flour
1/2 cup butter or margarine

In a large bowl combine 1/2 cup of butter and the cream cheese, and let come to room temperature. Add 2 cups of flour, and blend well. Chill. Roll out half of the dough and place in a 9-inch pie plate. Reserve the remaining dough for the top crust.

In a saucepan combine the remaining ingredients and bring to a boil. Pour the mixture into the crust. Roll out the remaining crust and place over the filling. Cut slits in the top crust to allow steam to escape. Bake in a 350° oven for 45 minutes.

Serves 6 to 8.

Patsy Curtis—Charlotte, Tennessee

Homemade love

Aunt Bee gives Opie his priorities:

AUNT BEE: Remember, first you eat the sandwiches and then you eat the apple pie. Not the apple pie and then the sandwiches. Do you understand?

OPIE: Yeah, I understand, even if it don't seem right.

AUNT BEE: Why doesn't it seem right?

OPIE: Well, if you get full before you finish, I'd sure rather leave over the sandwich than the pie.

AUNT BEE: I know, and that's exactly why I want you to do it the other way, and don't you forget it.

OPIE: O.K., Aunt Bee. Can I have my nickel for milk?

AUNT BEE: Uh-huh. Now remember this is for milk, not another piece of apple pie. You need that milk to make your bones hard.

AUNT BEE: (To Andy) That boy, I declare he's got the sweetest tooth I ever saw. You know, if he had his way, what he'd want for lunch? Two slices of apple pie between two pieces of apple pie and a slab of apple pie for dessert.

ANDY: Now that's not surprising, Aunt Bee, considering the green thumb you've got for apple pies.

AUNT BEE: Nonsense. He's just apple pie crazy.

Mom's Apple Pie in Paper Bag

A towsack full of love.

3 to 4 large cooking apples
1/2 cup sugar
2 tablespoons all-purpose flour
1/2 teaspoon nutmeg
Cinnamon to taste

1 9-inch unbaked pie shell
2 tablespoons lemon juice
1/2 cup sugar
1/2 cup all-purpose flour
1/2 cup butter or margarine

Peel the apples if desired. Quarter and then halve the apples to make chunks. In a large bowl combine the apple chunks, 1/2 cup of sugar, 2 tablespoons of flour, nutmeg, and cinnamon, tossing to coat the apples. Place the mixture in the pie shell, and pour lemon juice over all. Combine the remaining ingredients and sprinkle over the apple mixture. Slide the pie into a large paper bag (do not use one that has been recycled) and fold the open end over twice. Fasten with paper clips. Place the bag on a cookie sheet. Bake in a 425° oven for 1 hour. Be sure the bag does not touch the element. Slit the bag and cool the pie on a rack.

Serves 6 to 8.

Nancy Clark—Greensboro, North Carolina

Aunt Bee's Blueberry Pie

$2/3$ cup sugar
3 tablespoons all-purpose flour
$1/4$ teaspoon cinnamon

1 14-ounce can blueberries, juice drained
  and reserved
1 tablespoon butter
Pastry for 8-inch 2-crust pie

In a saucepan combine the sugar, flour, and cinnamon. Add the blueberry juice and cook over medium heat, stirring constantly, until the mixture boils. Remove from the heat and gently stir in the blueberries. Pour the filling into the crust and dot with butter. Cover with the top crust. Cut several slits in the pastry to allow the steam to escape. Turn the edges of the top crust under the lower crust edge and press around the rim with the tines of a fork. Bake in a 425° oven for 35 to 40 minutes, or until the pastry is nicely browned and the juice begins to bubble through the slits in the crust. Serve warm, topped with cream or ice cream.

Serves 6.

Lessons for Leon

Opie and Leon's Favorite Buttermilk Pie

2 cups sugar

1 teaspoon cinnamon

1 teaspoon nutmeg

1 teaspoon vanilla extract

2 tablespoons cornstarch

1/2 cup butter, melted

3 large eggs

1 cup buttermilk

1 9-inch pie shell

In a large bowl combine the sugar, cinnamon, nutmeg, vanilla, cornstarch, butter, and eggs. Beat with an electric mixer on low speed until well blended and uniform. Add the buttermilk and mix well. Pour into the pie shell. Bake in a 350° oven for 40 minutes, or until set and brown on the top.

Serves 6 to 8.

Mrs. Rance Howard (Ron and Clint's mom)—cast member

Al Becker's Butterscotch Pie

If you don't know Al Becker, it's not nearly as good.

4 tablespoons all-purpose flour

1 cup brown sugar

1/4 teaspoon salt

2 cups half-and-half, scalded

3 eggs separated

4 tablespoons butter (do not substitute)

1 teaspoon vanilla extract

1/4 teaspoon salt

6 tablespoons sugar

1 9-inch baked pie crust

174

In a saucepan combine the flour, brown sugar, and 1/4 teaspoon of salt. Gradually add the half-and-half, and cook over medium heat. Stir constantly until the mixture thickens and boils. Cook for 2 minutes. Remove from the heat and stir occasionally. Cool for a few minutes. Add a small amount of the filling mixture to the egg yolks, blend well, and add the egg mixture back to the filling mixture. Cook for 3 minutes, stirring constantly. Add the butter and 1/2 teaspoon of vanilla, and cool. Pour into the baked crust.

Beat the egg whites with 1/4 teaspoon of salt and 1/2 teaspoon of vanilla until frothy. Gradually add 6 tablespoons of sugar, beating well after each addition. Beat until stiff peaks form. Spread on the pie. Bake in a 350° oven for 12 to 15 minutes.

Serves 6 to 8.

Nancy Clark—Greensboro, North Carolina

Honest Cherry Pie

No lie, it's a treat.

1/2 cup butter
1 cup self-rising flour
1 cup sugar

1 cup milk
1 21-ounce can cherry pie filling

In a baking dish melt the butter. In a bowl combine the flour, sugar, and milk. Spread the cherry pie filling over the butter in the baking dish. Spoon the flour mixture over the cherries. Bake in a 350° oven until the crust is brown.

Serves 6.

Johnnie Bucy—Lebanon, Tennessee

When Opie appears to have made good marks in school, everyone shares the rewards:

ANDY: We're having a little celebration—kind of a pie celebration. Set down and have some.

BARNEY: No, thanks.

AUNT BEE: Oh, come on, pull up a chair.

BARNEY: No, I couldn't, really.

AUNT BEE: Oh, come on, Barney.

BARNEY: No, I couldn't.

ANDY: It's butterscotch pecan.

BARNEY: Well, seeing as how it's a celebration . . .

AUNT BEE: Come on, Opie. Show me how big a piece you want.

OPIE: *Big!*

Clara's Caramel Pie

1 cup packed brown sugar
1/2 cup sugar
2 teaspoons all-purpose flour
2 level teaspoons cornmeal

3 egg yolks
2 cups milk
1/4 cup margarine
1 9-inch baked pie shell

In a saucepan combine the brown sugar, sugar, flour, cornmeal, egg yolks, milk, and margarine. Cook until thick. It takes about 25 to 30 minutes of stirring for it to boil down. Pour the filling into the baked pie shell, and you'll have the best pie you ever had. You can't miss.

Variation: You can add a meringue topping to this with your 3 egg whites and 6 tablespoons of sugar. Beat until fluffy. Spread over the pie and place under the broiler until browned.

Serves 6 to 8.

Lois Rogers—Readyville, Tennessee

Andy's Chocolate Eggnog Layer Pie

True justice of the pieces.

1 envelope unflavored gelatin
1/2 cup cold water
1/3 cup sugar
2 tablespoons cornstarch
1/4 teaspoon salt
2 cups commercial eggnog
1 1/2 squares unsweetened chocolate, melted

1 teaspoon vanilla extract
1 9-inch baked pie shell
1 teaspoon rum extract
2 cups whipping cream
1/4 cup confectioners' sugar
Chocolate curls (optional)

In a small bowl soften the gelatin in the water. Set aside. In a 1-quart saucepan combine the sugar, cornstarch, and salt. Gradually stir in the eggnog. Cook over medium heat, stirring constantly, until thickened. Cook for 2 minutes. Remove from the heat and add the gelatin mixture, stirring until dissolved.

Divide the filling in half, setting half aside to cool. Add the melted chocolate and vanilla to half, stir well, and pour into the pie shell. Chill until set.

Add rum extract to the remaining filling. Whip 1 cup of cream and fold into the cooled mixture. Spoon over the chocolate layer and chill.

Whip the remaining cream and add the confectioners' sugar. Spread over the pie, or pipe from a pastry bag, and garnish with chocolate curls, if desired.

Serves 6 to 8.

Tanya Jones—Mount Airy, North Carolina

> *How to find a prison escapee in Mayberry:*
>
> **ANDY:** If I was a criminal and I was heading through them woods, I'd stop off at Emma Brand's house.
>
> **BARNEY:** You would?
>
> **ANDY:** For sure. Now, you know there ain't a day goes by that Emma don't make a batch of pies and put 'em in the window to cool. Well, you know it's pretty hard on the average fellow to pass by without sniffin' and a-hungerin' for a slice of pie. You can just imagine what that's gonna do to a starvin' escapee. Yeah. Let's go on over there.

St. Benedict's Coconut Cream Pie

A dream come true.

1 cup sugar
1/2 cup all-purpose flour
1/4 teaspoon salt
3 cups milk
4 eggs, separated
3 tablespoons butter or margarine

1 1/2 teaspoons vanilla extract
1 3 1/2-ounce can flaked coconut
1 9-inch baked pie shell
1 teaspoon vanilla extract
1/2 teaspoon cream of tartar
1/2 cup sugar

In a saucepan combine 1 cup of sugar, the flour, and salt. Gradually stir in the milk. Cook, stirring constantly, until thickened and bubbly. Reduce the heat and cook, stirring constantly, for 2 minutes more. Remove from the heat.

Beat the egg yolks slightly. Gradually stir 1 cup of the hot mixture into the egg yolks. Return the egg yolk mixture to the saucepan and bring to a gentle boil. Cook and stir for 2 minutes. Remove from the heat. Stir in the butter and vanilla. Stir in 1 cup of the coconut. Pour the mixture into the baked pie shell.

Beat the egg whites with the vanilla and cream of tartar. Gradually add 1/2 cup of sugar, beating until stiff. Spread over the hot filling, sealing to the edges of the crust. Sprinkle with the remaining coconut. Bake in a 350° oven for 12 to 15 minutes, or until the meringue is golden. Cool. Cover and refrigerate until ready to serve.

Serves 6 to 8.

Opie's Chocolate Pie

This is what puts the "pie" in Opie.

1 1/2 cups sugar

2 tablespoons all-purpose flour

3 tablespoons cocoa

3 egg yolks, slightly beaten

1 teaspoon vanilla extract

1 cup sweetened condensed milk

1 9-inch unbaked pie shell

3 egg whites

6 to 7 tablespoons sugar

In a bowl combine 1 1/2 cups of sugar, the flour, and cocoa. Add the beaten egg yolks, vanilla, and milk. Pour the mixture into the pie shell. Bake in a 425° oven for 10 minutes. Reduce the heat to 350° and bake for 25 to 30 minutes.

Beat the egg whites with 6 to 7 tablespoons of sugar until stiff. Spread onto the cooked pie, and brown under a broiler for 2 to 3 minutes.

Serves 6 to 8.

Hazel Beck—North Little Rock, Arkansas

"Shazam!"

Campbell Cranberry Pie

2³/₄ cup cranberries
2 cups sugar
2 teaspoons cornstarch

4 tablespoons all-purpose flour
¹/₂ cup brandy or orange juice
Pastry for 8-inch 2-crust pie

In a large bowl combine the cranberries, sugar, cornstarch, flour, and brandy. Turn the mixture into the pie crust and top with the remaining pastry. Bake in a 350° oven for 50 to 60 minutes.
Serves 6.

Hal and Louise Smith—cast member

Mr. Dave's Fudge "Browne" Pie

Opie says this magical dessert is "gollywobbler" good.

¹/₃ cup cocoa
1 cup sugar
¹/₂ cup butter
2 eggs

1 teaspoon vanilla extract
¹/₂ cup chopped nuts
2 tablespoons all-purpose flour
Ice cream

Grease a pie plate. In a saucepan melt the cocoa, sugar, and butter over low heat and stir until smooth. Add the eggs, vanilla, nuts, and flour. Stir until smooth. Pour the mixture into the prepared pie plate. Put the pie in a cold oven. Set the oven at 325° and bake for 25 minutes. Top with ice cream and serve.
Serves 6 to 8.

Robin and Tommy Ford—Northport, Alabama

Bee's Gooseberry Pie

Put some ice cream on top and you'll swallow your tongue, honey!

Wash some gooseberries and put some sugar on them. Boil them on the stove. Roll out a crust and put it in a pie plate. Put the berries in the crust and fold over the ends. Dot with butter and sprinkle with sugar. Bake in a 450° oven until done.
Serves 6 to 8.

Lois Rogers—Readyville, Tennessee

Grand Grasshopper Pie

1½ cups finely crushed chocolate wafers	2 tablespoons white crème de cacao
6 tablespoons butter or margarine, melted	2 cups whipping cream
6½ cups miniature marshmallows	Unsweetened whipped cream
¼ cup milk	Chocolate curls
¼ cup green crème de menthe	

In a bowl combine the crushed chocolate wafers and butter. Turn into a 9-inch pie plate and press evenly onto the bottom and sides. Chill for about 1 hour or until firm.

In a large saucepan combine the marshmallows and milk. Cook over low heat, stirring constantly, until the marshmallows are melted. Remove from the heat. Cool the mixture, stirring every 5 minutes. Add the crème de menthe and crème de cacao. In a large bowl whip 2 cups of whipping cream until soft peaks form. Fold the marshmallow mixture into the whipped cream. Turn into the chilled crust. Freeze for several hours or overnight, until firm.

Before serving, garnish with whipped cream and chocolate curls.
Serves 6 to 8.

Clara's Nesselrode Pie

Perfect dessert for the garden club or after choir practice.

1 tablespoon unflavored gelatin	6 tablespoons sugar
¼ cup cold water	2 tablespoons rum
2 eggs, separated	1 9-inch baked pie shell
¼ cup sugar	Whipped cream
2 cups light cream	Grated sweet chocolate

In a small bowl soak the gelatin in the cold water for about 5 minutes. In a separate bowl beat the egg yolks. Add ¼ cup of sugar and the cream. In a saucepan heat the egg yolk mixture and cook until smooth and slightly thickened. Add the gelatin mixture and stir until dissolved. Chill until the mixture just begins to set.

Beat the egg whites until they hold a peak. Gradually add 6 tablespoons of sugar and beat well. Fold into the chilled mixture and add the rum. Pour the mixture into the pie shell and refrigerate for 3 to 4 hours. Serve with whipped cream and sprinkle with grated chocolate.
Serves 6 to 8.

Susan Burgesser—Dover, Minnesota

Hubcaps Lesch's Lemon Chess Pie

You'll love this one a great deal.

2 eggs	Juice and grated rind of 1 lemon
1 tablespoon cornmeal	3 tablespoons milk
1/4 cup butter	Pinch salt
1 cup sugar	1 9-inch unbaked pie shell

In a bowl combine the eggs, cornmeal, butter, sugar, lemon juice and grated rind, milk, and salt. Pour the mixture into the pie shell. Bake in a 400° oven for about 25 minutes, or until the filling is just set and the crust and filling are browned.

Serves 6 to 8.

Charlotte Womack—Browns Summit, North Carolina

Opie's Lemonade Pie

Opie takes his stand for this one.

1 8-ounce carton Cool Whip	1 14-ounce can sweetened condensed milk
1 6-ounce can frozen lemonade concentrate	1 9-inch graham cracker crust

In a large bowl combine the Cool Whip, lemonade, and sweetened condensed milk, blending well. Pour the mixture into the crust and chill until firm, about 2 hours.

Serves 6 to 8.

Freida Crawley—Nashville, Tennessee

Carolina Peach Basket Pie

They'll travel from the four corners for this one.

4 cups peeled and sliced peaches	1/4 teaspoon salt
2 tablespoons all-purpose flour	1 9-inch unbaked pie shell
1/2 teaspoon nutmeg	1 cup cream

In a large bowl toss the peaches with the flour, nutmeg, and salt. Turn the mixture into the pie shell. Pour the cream over the top. Bake in a 350° oven for 35 to 40 minutes.

Serves 6 to 8.

Hazel Beck—North Little Rock, Arkansas

Mt. Pilot Pecan Pie

A true Southern delicacy.

1 cup dark corn syrup	1 cup sugar
3 eggs, slightly beaten	2 tablespoons margarine, melted
1/8 teaspoon salt	1 cup pecans, chopped or halved
1 teaspoon vanilla	1 9-inch unbaked pie shell

In a large bowl combine all of the ingredients except the pie shell, adding the pecans last. Pour the mixture into the pie shell. Bake in a 400° oven for 15 minutes. Reduce the heat to 350° and bake for 30 to 35 minutes. The pie is done when the outer edge of the filling is set and the center is slightly soft.

Serves 6 to 8.

Hazel Beck—North Little Rock, Arkansas

Praline Pumpkin Pie Juanita

It's a pleasure to serve.

1 cup graham cracker crumbs	3 tablespoons sugar
1/2 cup ground filberts	6 tablespoons butter

In a small bowl combine all of the ingredients. Press the mixture into a 9-inch pie plate. Bake in a 375° oven for 6 to 8 minutes. Cool.

1 envelope unflavored gelatin	1 teaspoon cinnamon
1/2 cup sugar	1/2 teaspoon salt
4 eggs, separated	1/4 teaspoon cloves
1/2 cup praline liqueur	1/8 teaspoon cream of tartar
1/4 cup melted margarine	3/4 cup cream, whipped
1 16-ounce can pumpkin	Whipped cream for garnish
1/2 cup brown sugar	Crumbled brickle

In a saucepan combine the gelatin and sugar. In a small bowl beat together the egg yolks, praline liqueur, and melted margarine. Add the mixture to the gelatin mixture and let stand for 1 minute. Stir over low heat until the gelatin is dissolved, about 5 minutes. Blend in the pumpkin, brown sugar, cinnamon, salt, and cloves. Pour into a bowl and chill, stirring occasionally, until the mixture mounds when dropped from a spoon.

Beat the egg whites to soft peaks. Gradually add the cream of tartar and beat until stiff. Fold the egg whites, and then the whipped cream, into the pumpkin mixture. Turn three-fourths of the mixture into the crust. Chill until almost set. Spoon on the remaining mixture, and chill until firm. Serve with whipped cream and bits of brickle as topping.

Serves 6 to 8.

Nancy Clark—Greensboro, North Carolina

Double Pumpkin Pies

So good you'll be glad you made two.

6 eggs	2 teaspoons pumpkin pie spice
2 cups packed brown sugar	4 cups pumpkin
2 cups sugar	1 1/3 cups evaporated milk
4 tablespoons all-purpose flour	1 teaspoon salt
2 teaspoons nutmeg	2 9-inch unbaked pie shells

In a large bowl beat the eggs until well beaten. Add the brown sugar and blend well. In a separate bowl sift together the sugar, flour, nutmeg, and pumpkin pie spice, so the spices won't be lumpy. Add the sugar-spice mixture to the egg mixture. Blend the mixture into the pumpkin. Add the milk and salt. Turn the filling into the pie shells. Bake in a 400° oven for a few minutes, reduce the heat to 300°, and bake until a knife inserted in the center comes out clean.

Serves 6 to 8.

Mrs. Tommie Rogers—Woodbury, Tennessee

Aunt Bee's Blue Ribbon Rhubarb Pie

3 1/2 cups rhubarb, cut up	2 egg yolks
9-inch 2-crust unbaked pie shell	1/2 teaspoon salt
1 1/4 cups sugar	1/2 teaspoon cinnamon
4 tablespoons all-purpose flour	2 tablespoons melted butter

Place the rhubarb in the pie shell. In a bowl combine the remaining ingredients and spread evenly over the rhubarb. Cover and top with strips of crust. Bake in a 425° oven for 15 minutes. Reduce the heat to 350° and bake for 45 minutes, until done.

Serves 6 to 8.

Jennifer Trumbull—Nashville, Tennessee

Mayberry Strawberry Pie

Berry, berry good.

2 pints fresh strawberries, washed and
   hulled
1 cup sugar
4 tablespoons all-purpose flour

1 cup water
1 9-inch baked pie shell
Whipped cream

In a saucepan mash about 5 or 6 ripe berries, and combine with the sugar, flour, and water. Cook until thick, and refrigerate until cold.

   Just before serving, place the strawberries in the pie shell, reserving a few for garnish. Pour the glaze over the berries. Cover with whipped cream and garnish with the reserved berries. Slice and serve.

   Serves 6 to 8.

Mary Ellis—Albuquerque, New Mexico

Tears on Your Pillow Pie

A sweet tooth pleaser.

1/3 cup butter, melted
1 1/2 cups brown sugar
2 eggs

1 tablespoon all-purpose flour
1/2 cup evaporated milk
1 9-inch unbaked pie shell

In a large bowl beat together the butter, brown sugar, eggs, flour, and milk until well blended. Pour the filling into the pie shell. Bake in a 350° oven for 35 minutes. Turn off the oven and leave the pie for 45 minutes to 1 hour.

   Serves 6 to 8.

Sherry Hyatt—Kingsport, Tennessee

Frank Myers's Blackberry Cobbler

Never out of season.

3/4 quart fresh or frozen blackberries
11/4 cups sugar
2 heaping tablespoons cornstarch
1/2 teaspoon salt
1/4 cup sherry
Pastry for 9-inch 2-crust deep-dish pie

In a saucepan combine the blackberries and just enough water to prevent sticking. Bring slowly to a boil. Add 1 cup of sugar and continue to heat. In a small bowl combine 1/4 cup of sugar, the cornstarch, salt, and sherry. If the mixture is thick, use a small amount of liquid from the berry mixture to make a thinner consistency. Add to the berry mixture. Cook until the sauce just begins to thicken. Pour into the pie crust. Cut the remaining pastry into strips and form a lattice top over the filling. Bake in a 375° oven for 15 to 20 minutes, until the top is lightly browned.

Serves 6.

John Masters's Mincemeat

Measures up to anything.

11/2 pounds beef
11/2 pounds pork
1/2 pound suet
2 pounds seedless raisins
2 pounds currants
2 pounds sugar
1 pound brown sugar
2 oranges
2 lemons
1/2 pound citron
2 quarts chopped apples
1 cup molasses
2 teaspoons ground cloves
3 teaspoons cinnamon
3 teaspoons ginger
1 teaspoon nutmeg
1 cup cider

In a large stock pot cook the beef, pork, and suet until tender. Mince or grind through a food grinder. In a saucepan cook the raisins and currants until tender in water to cover. Drain. Finely chop the oranges, lemons, citron, and apples, or grind through a food grinder. In a large saucepan combine the meat, raisins and currants, and remaining ingredients. Simmer together in water to cover for 12 minutes. Put into sterile jars and seal while hot.

To make a pie, fill an unbaked pie shell with about 3 cups of mincemeat. Cover with a top crust. Bake in a 425° oven for 15 minutes. Reduce the temperature to 375° and continue to bake for 35 minutes.

Makes 7 quarts, enough for about 9 pies.

Janie Love—Hermitage, Tennessee

Opie's No-Fail Pie Dough

What filling to add is up to you.

3 cups all-purpose flour
1 1/2 teaspoons salt
2 tablespoons sugar
1 1/4 cups shortening

1 egg, slightly beaten
6 tablespoons cold water
1 tablespoon vinegar

In a bowl combine the flour, salt, and sugar. Cut the shortening into the flour mixture until crumbly. Beat the egg, add water and vinegar to the egg, and blend the mixture into the flour mixture until all of the flour is moist. Don't overbeat. Sometimes it's a good idea to let the mixture rest for 10 minutes to ensure tenderness.

Makes pastry for a 2-crust pie.

Susan Ryman—Houston, Texas

Loafers Lemon Lotus Ice Cream

First tasted at Justine's in Atlanta.

4 quarts half-and-half
6 cups plus 7 tablespoons sugar
Grated rind of 10 lemons
2 cups lemon juice

2 teaspoons vanilla extract
1 teaspoon almond extract
2 cups chopped almonds, lightly toasted

A day ahead of serving, combine all of the ingredients except the almonds. This allows the flavors to blend. Add the nuts just before freezing. Pour the mixture into a freezer and prepare according to the manufacturer's directions.

Serves 8 to 10.

Nancy Clark—Greensboro, North Carolina

Jud and Choney's Mud Ice Cream

Check 'er out.

2 quarts half-and-half
2 14-ounce cans sweetened condensed milk
1 teaspoon vanilla extract

1 6-ounce box instant chocolate pudding mix
2 cups chopped pecans

In a large bowl combine all of the ingredients. Pour the mixture into a freezer and prepare according to the manufacturer's directions.

Serves 6 to 8.

Bobby E. Thompson Jr.—Manvel, Texas

COUSIN BRADFORD: It has a magic quality—it's ambrosia.

Opie's Oreo Ice Cream

This is the way the cookie crumbles.

6 eggs
1 1/2 cups sugar
1 14-ounce can sweetened condensed milk
1 quart half-and-half

1 pint whipping cream
1 20-ounce package Oreo cookies, crushed
Milk

Beat the eggs until thick. Add the sugar and beat until creamy, about 15 minutes. Add the sweetened condensed milk, half-and-half, and cream. Fold in the crushed cookies. Pour the mixture into a freezer and finish filling the container with milk. Prepare according to the manufacturer's directions.

Makes 1 1/2 gallons.

Patsy Curtis—Charlotte, Tennessee

More front porch conversation:
    ANDY: You know what I believe I'll do? Run down to the drugstore and get some ice cream for later.
    BARNEY: You want me to go? I'll go.
    ANDY: No, I'll go.
    BARNEY: I don't mind going.
    ANDY: I don't either. I can go.
    BARNEY: You're probably tired. Why don't you let me go?
    ANDY: No, I'm not tired. I'll go.
    BARNEY: I sure don't mind going.
    ANDY: Why don't we both just go?
    BARNEY: O.K.
    ANDY: You ready?
    BARNEY: Uh-huh.
        (Both rise slowly.)
    BARNEY: Where we goin'?
    ANDY: Down to the drugstore to get some ice cream for later.

Cousin Bradford's Strawberry Ice Cream

The stuff dreams are made of.

Juice of 3 oranges
Juice of 3 lemons
3 cups sugar
3 cups milk

1¹/₂ cups heavy cream
1¹/₂ cups light cream
2 10-ounce packages frozen strawberries

In a large bowl combine all of the ingredients. Freeze in an ice cream freezer according to the manufacturer's instructions.

Makes about 2 quarts of ice cream.

Thelma Lou's Chocolate Cream Dessert

¹/₃ to ¹/₂ cup semisweet chocolate chips
1 tablespoon water

3 eggs, separated
Heavy cream or whipped cream

In a double boiler over simmering water, melt the chocolate with the water, stirring until smooth. Remove from the heat and add the egg yolks one at a time, beating well after each addition. Beat the egg whites until stiff and fold gently into the chocolate mixture. Spoon lightly into sherbet glasses. Chill.

Serve with heavy cream or whipped cream, flavored with rum or vanilla.

Serves 4 to 6.

Betty Lynn—cast member

Siler City Peach Cream Freeze

Sweeter than a spoonful of honey.

1 21-ounce can peach pie filling
1 14-ounce can sweetened condensed milk
1 20-ounce can crushed pineapple, drained

¹/₄ cup lemon juice
1 cup chopped pecans
1 8-ounce carton Cool Whip

Combine all of the ingredients, adding Cool Whip last. Freeze the mixture until firm.

Serves 6 to 8.

Vickie Russell—Siler City, North Carolina

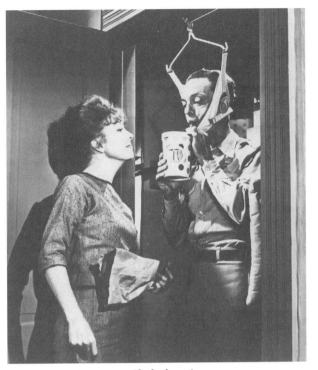

Shakedown!

On the front porch:

OPIE: Paw, what'd they do 'fore they had 'frigerators?

ANDY: They had ice boxes. Boy, those were the days. Too bad you missed 'em. I remember hot days like this, old ice wagon'd come by. Us boys would chase after it, jump on the back of it, snitch a piece of ice. Always a little sawdust sticking to it. Nothin' like the taste of wet sawdust from the bottom of the wagon. Something's gone out of life since then. You know that, Aunt Bee?

AUNT BEE: Uh-huh. Typhoid.

OPIE: Before ice boxes what'd they do?

ANDY: They had cold cellars, places where they kept things cold.

OPIE: Before cold cellars, what did they do?

ANDY: They had the Ice Age.

OPIE: Oh.

ANDY: Now don't ask me what they had 'fore the Ice Age. That's before my time. Just set around and cuss the weather, I reckon. Used to we'd set around and cuss the weather. Now we cuss the ice box.

Goob to the last drop

Clara's Fabulous Flaming Christmas Pudding

Fare with flair.

2 cups sifted all-purpose flour	1/2 cup sugar
1 teaspoon baking powder	4 eggs
1 teaspoon cinnamon	1 pound dates, chopped
1 teaspoon allspice	Oil
1 teaspoon nutmeg	Sugar
1/2 teaspoon cloves	Lemon extract
1/2 cup butter	

Prepare a 1 1/2-quart pudding mold or two 1-pound coffee tins by rolling oil in them, draining, and sprinkling the inside with sugar.

In a large bowl, stir together the flour, baking powder, cinnamon, allspice, nutmeg, and cloves. With an electric mixer cream the butter and sugar together. Add the eggs one at a time, beating after each addition. Add the dates, and beat well. Blend in the dry ingredients. Turn the batter into the prepared mold. If the mold does not have its own top, fashion one from several layers of aluminum foil, and tie securely with string. Place the mold on a rack in a large kettle and add boiling water to a depth of $3/4$ the height of the mold. Cover the kettle and gently boil the pudding for 3 hours, replenishing the water as needed.

Turn out onto a rack to cool. The pudding may be frozen or stored for several weeks in the refrigerator.

$1/2$ cup sugar	Raisins
2 tablespoons cornstarch	Pecans
1 cup hot water	1 pint whipping cream
1 egg, beaten	4 tablespoons sugar
Pinch salt	$1/2$ teaspoon vanilla extract
2 tablespoons butter	Sugar cubes
Red and green maraschino cherries	Lemon extract
Pineapple chunks	

In a saucepan combine the sugar and cornstarch. Add the hot water, beaten egg, and salt. Cook over medium heat, stirring constantly, until thickened. Drop in the butter and stir until melted. Add the fruit and pecans. Pour the sauce into a serving container.

Beat the cream and gradually add 4 tablespoons of sugar. Fold in the vanilla. Be careful not to overheat as the cream will turn to butter.

Drop the sugar cubes briefly in lemon extract. Place the pudding on a serving platter, and surround with the sugar cubes, placing several on top of the pudding. Light the cubes, and bring the flaming pudding into the dining room.

Slice the pudding at the table, spoon on the sauce, and top with the whipped cream.
Serves 12.

Alice Ewing—Franklin, Tennessee

Lemon Fluffy

It's the cat's.

1 3-ounce package lemon gelatin	1 13-ounce can evaporated milk, chilled
1 cup hot water	$1/2$ teaspoon salt
1 cup sugar	1 cup crushed vanilla wafers
$1/4$ cup lemon juice	

In a bowl dissolve the gelatin in the hot water. Add the sugar and lemon juice. Mix well and chill until slightly congealed. Beat the chilled milk at high speed until very fluffy, adding the salt while beating. Slowly fold the milk into the slightly congealed gelatin until well mixed.

Line a 9 x 13-inch pan with the crushed vanilla wafers. Turn the gelatin mixture into the pan over the wafer crumbs and chill thoroughly.
Serves 12.

Mary Clark—Nashville, Tennessee

Hickory Holler Persimmon Pudding

2 cups persimmon pulp
2 cups sugar
2 eggs, beaten
1¾ cups all-purpose flour
2 teaspoons baking powder
1 cup half-and-half

1 cup buttermilk
1 teaspoon baking soda
⅓ cup butter or margarine
1 teaspoon cinnamon
1 teaspoon vanilla extract

In a large bowl combine the persimmon pulp, sugar, and eggs. In a separate bowl sift the flour with the baking powder. In a small bowl combine the half-and-half and the buttermilk, and add the baking soda. Add the flour mixture to the persimmon mixture alternately with the buttermilk mixture, stirring well after each addition.

Place the butter in a 9 x 13-inch cake pan and place in a 325° oven until melted. Using a pastry brush, coat the sides of the pan. Pour the excess butter into the batter. Add the cinnamon and vanilla, and mix well. Pour into the pan. Bake in a 325° oven for 1 hour or until a table knife inserted in the center comes out clean. The pudding will puff up and then flatten as it cooks.

Variations: Some cooks add nuts, raisins, or coconut before baking.
Serves 12.

Grace Farrar—Lebanon, Tennessee

Goober's No Shoes and Rice Pudding

Perfect for any occasion.

1 cup uncooked instant rice
5 eggs
½ cup sugar
½ teaspoon salt

1 teaspoon vanilla extract
½ to 1 teaspoon nutmeg or cinnamon
4 cups milk, scalded

Prepare the rice according to the package directions. In a mixing bowl beat the eggs, and add the sugar, salt, vanilla, and nutmeg. Mix well. Add the scalded milk and stir well. Place the cooked rice in a 2-quart baking dish. Pour the egg mixture over the rice, and stir to blend. Place the baking dish in a cake or similar pan and pour ½ to 1 inch of hot water into the larger pan. Bake in a 350° oven for 30 to 40 minutes or until a knife inserted in the middle comes out clean.

Variations: The pudding may be sprinkled with cinnamon or nutmeg, and raisins or currants may also be added if desired.
Serves 4 to 6.

Margaret Adams—Chicago, Illinois

Puddin' Tame Tapioca Pudding

Ask me again and I'll tell you the same.

1/2 cup tapioca
3 cups milk
1/4 teaspoon salt

1/3 cup plus 2 tablespoons sugar
2 eggs, separated
1/2 teaspoon vanilla extract

In a saucepan soak the tapioca in 1/2 cup of milk for 20 minutes. Add the remaining milk and the salt, and bring to a boil. Add the sugar slowly, and reduce the heat to the lowest setting. Simmer for 5 minutes.

In a large bowl combine the egg yolks and a small amount of the hot tapioca mixture. Stir carefully to prevent curdling. Add the yolk mixture to the saucepan. Bring the mixture to a boil, stirring constantly. Reduce the heat to the lowest setting and cook for 3 more minutes. Remove from the heat.

Beat the egg whites and slowly add the hot mixture. Add the vanilla. Serve the pudding warm or chilled.

Serves 6.

Andy and Barney make an impression at the Esquire Club in Raleigh:
ANDY: This is good, Roger. What is it?
ROGER: It's Baked Alaska.
ANDY: I don't believe I ever heard of it.
BARNEY: Sure you have, Andy. You just forgot. That's Baked Alaska. It's that new dessert that come out since it become a state.

Esquire Club Baked Alaska

Sponge cake or layer cake
5 egg whites, stiffly beaten
2/3 cup sugar

1 quart Neapolitan ice cream
Sugar

Trim the sponge cake to measure 1 inch larger on all sides than the ice cream. Place on a wooden cutting board.

Add the sugar to the beaten egg whites, and beat until stiff peaks form. Place the ice cream on top of the trimmed sponge cake. Spread the meringue over the ice cream, carefully sealing to the edges of the cake. Sprinkle the top of the meringue with sugar for a sparkle effect. Bake in a 450° oven for about 5 minutes, until golden brown. Slide from the board onto a serving platter, and slice in front of guests.

Serves 6.

Mary Ann McNeese—Nashville, Tennessee

Bee's Baked Apples

Appealing for all.

4 to 6 apples (York are excellent)
3 cups water

1 cup sugar
1/3 cup orange juice

Peel, split, and core the apples. Place in a frying pan and add the water and sugar. Bring the mixture to a boil. Cook until the apples begin to look clear. Lift the apples from the frying pan and place in an ovenproof glass baking dish. To the sugar and water mixture add the orange juice. Cook the mixture down until only 1 cup remains. Pour over the apples. Bake in a 350° oven for 30 minutes.

Serves 4 to 6.

Louise Davidson—Charlotte, North Carolina

Curried Harvest Ball Fruit

Autumn—eat 'em.

2 12-ounce packages mixed dried fruit
2 13 1/4-ounce cans pineapple chunks
2 21-ounce cans cherry pie filling

1 cup dry sherry (or apple cider)
1/2 cup water
2 to 4 teaspoons curry powder

Cut the large pieces of dried fruit in half. In a 4-quart casserole dish combine the dried fruit and undrained pineapple chunks. In a bowl combine the pie filling, sherry, water, and curry powder, and pour over the fruit. Cover and bake in a 350° oven for 1 hour.

Serves 16.

Blanche Cox—Florissant, Missouri

Billie's Blueberry Dessert

2 16-ounce packages fresh or frozen
    blueberries
1 egg, slightly beaten
1/3 cup sugar

1 teaspoon grated orange rind
2 tablespoons lemon juice
1/2 cup graham cracker crumbs
Whipped cream or ice cream

Butter a 9-inch baking dish. In a large bowl combine all of the ingredients except the whipped cream or ice cream. Pour into the prepared dish. Bake in a 350° oven for 25 minutes. Serve with whipped cream or ice cream.

Serves 6.

Everett and Deane Ward Greenbaum—writer

Newton Monroe's Pineapple Casserole

If need be, you can buy a two-dollar pineapple skinner from Newton—
just like the one Barney gave Thelma Lou for her birthday.

2 20-ounce cans chunk unsweetened
  pineapple, drained
3/4 cup sugar
5 tablespoons all-purpose flour

1 3/4 cups grated cheddar cheese
3/4 cup crushed Ritz crackers
1/2 cup butter, melted

Grease a large ovenproof bowl. Pour the pineapple into the prepared bowl. Combine
the sugar and flour, and sprinkle over the pineapple. Sprinkle the grated cheese over the
pineapple, then the cracker crumbs. Pour the butter over the top. Bake in a 350° oven for
30 minutes.
    Serves 6 to 8.

Sherry Hyatt—Kingsport, Tennessee

Checkers Chocolate Sauce

The crowning touch.

1/4 cup margarine
1 1/2 squares unsweetened chocolate, cut
  into small bits
1/4 cup cocoa

3/4 cup sugar
1/4 cup cream or milk
1/8 teaspoon salt
1 teaspoon vanilla extract

In a saucepan melt the butter and chocolate over low heat until smooth. Stir in the cocoa,
sugar, cream, and salt. Bring slowly to a boil, but do not stir. Remove from the heat and
blend in the vanilla. Serve warm.
    Makes 1 1/2 cups.

Lemon Glaze Otis

3 tablespoons milk
2 tablespoons butter
2 cups sifted confectioners' sugar

1 teaspoon grated lemon rind (or orange)
1/2 teaspoon lemon juice

In a saucepan heat the milk and butter over low heat, stirring constantly until the butter
melts. In a bowl combine the confectioners' sugar and the heated milk mixture. Stir until
smooth. Stir in the lemon rind and lemon juice. Especially good for angel food cake.
    Makes about 1/2 cup.

Jane Ellis—Albuquerque, New Mexico

Kooky cutter

Cookies and Candies

Barney's Banana Granola Cookies

1/2 cup butter or margarine, softened
1 cup firmly packed brown sugar
1 egg
1/2 teaspoon vanilla extract
1 cup mashed bananas

1 1/2 cups all-purpose flour
1 teaspoon cinnamon
1/2 teaspoon baking soda
1/2 teaspoon salt
1 cup granola

Grease 2 cookie sheets. In a large bowl cream the butter and brown sugar with an electric mixer at medium speed. Add the egg, vanilla, and bananas, beating until well blended. Add the flour, cinnamon, baking soda, and salt, and mix until blended. Stir in the granola. Drop by the tablespoon onto the prepared cookie sheets, spacing about 2 inches apart. Bake in a 375° oven for 12 minutes. Cool on a wire rack.

Makes about 4 dozen.

Harvey Bullock—writer

Jolly Good Chocolate Chip Cookies

A favorite with Opie and his merry men.

1/2 cup butter
6 tablespoons sugar
1 1/4 cups all-purpose flour
1/2 a beaten egg

Vanilla extract
1/4 cup chocolate chips
Rolled or jumbo oats

Lightly grease a cookie sheet. In a large bowl cream together the butter and sugar until light and fluffy. Add the flour, egg, and a few drops of vanilla. Beat well. Add the chocolate chips. Shape by hand into little balls, and roll in the oats. Place them on the prepared cookie sheet and press them down slightly. Bake in a 350° oven for 10 to 15 minutes, until golden brown. Remove from the tray while still hot and place on a wire rack to cool.

Makes up to 40 cookies, depending on how small you make them.

Karen Thomas—Manchester, England

Howie Pruitt's Supreme Chocolate Chip Cookies

2$^1/_2$ cups all-purpose flour
1 teaspoon baking soda
1 teaspoon salt
1 cup butter
$^3/_4$ cup sugar
$^3/_4$ cup brown sugar

1 teaspoon vanilla extract
2 eggs
1 12-ounce package chocolate chips
1 12-ounce package raisins
1 10-ounce package plain M&M candies

In a small bowl combine the flour, baking soda, and salt. Set aside. In a large bowl beat together the butter, sugar, brown sugar, and vanilla until creamy. Beat in the eggs. Gradually blend in the flour mixture. Stir in the chocolate chips and raisins. Drop by the tablespoon onto ungreased cookie sheets. Bake in a 375° oven for 9 to 11 minutes, until the edges are golden brown. Remove from the oven and place the M&M candies on top of the cookies while the cookies are still hot. Serve with cold milk.

   Makes about 3 dozen.

Dennis Rush—cast member

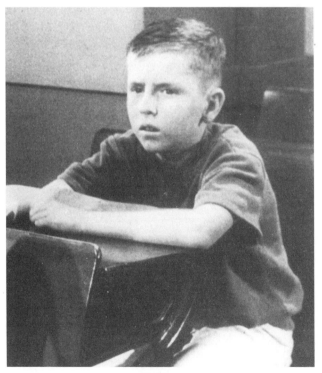

Howie

Ben Weaver's Christmas Cut-Out Cookies

Bound to put a smile on even a Scrooge's face.

1/2 cup butter	1/2 teaspoon vanilla extract
1 cup sugar	3 cups sifted all-purpose flour
2 eggs	1/2 teaspoon baking soda

In a large bowl cream the butter and sugar together until light. Add the eggs one at a time, beating well. Add the vanilla. In a separate bowl sift together the flour and baking soda, and add enough flour to the creamed mixture to form a dough that holds together. Chill for about 1 hour.

Roll the dough on a lightly floured surface to 1/8-inch thickness. Cut with cookie cutters. Place the cookies on an ungreased cookie sheet. Bake in a 350° oven for 8 to 10 minutes.

Makes 3 dozen.

Pat Rasmussen—Cokato, Minnesota

Juanita's Ginger Cookies

They're a snap.

3/4 cup shortening	2 cups all-purpose flour
1 cup sugar	3 teaspoons baking soda
4 tablespoons molasses	1 teaspoon cinnamon
1/4 teaspoon salt	1 teaspoon ginger
1 egg	1/2 teaspoon cloves

Grease a cookie sheet. In a large bowl cream together the shortening and sugar. Add the molasses, salt, and egg, and blend well. In a separate bowl sift together the dry ingredients. Blend into the creamed mixture. Shape the dough into small balls and roll in granulated sugar. Place on a greased cookie sheet. Bake in a 350° oven for 10 to 12 minutes.

Makes about 6 dozen.

Jane Ellis—Albuquerque, New Mexico

AUNT BEE: I took the liberty of making you a snack.

199

Harvey's Little Big Orange Cookies

1 cup butter, softened	1 teaspoon grated orange rind
1 cup sugar	1 1/2 cups sifted all-purpose flour
1 egg	1/2 teaspoon salt
1 1/2 teaspoons orange extract	

In a large bowl cream together the butter and sugar. Add the egg and the remaining ingredients. Drop by the spoonful onto an ungreased cookie sheet. Bake in a 375° oven for 10 minutes.

Makes 2 dozen.

Harvey Bullock—writer

Mr. No-Bake Cookies

They'll say lovin' with no oven.

1/2 cup margarine	1/2 cup peanut butter
4 tablespoons cocoa	3 cups quick oats
2 cups sugar	1/4 teaspoon vanilla extract
1/2 cup milk	Pinch salt

In a saucepan combine the margarine, cocoa, sugar, and milk. Bring the mixture to a boil, and boil for 1 minute. Remove from the burner, and add the remaining ingredients. Drop from a spoon onto waxed paper.

Makes about 3 dozen.

Terri Hamilton—Nashville, Tennessee

Bee's Biscochitos

Rio Grande biscuit cookies.

6 cups sifted all-purpose flour	2 teaspoons anise seed
3 teaspoons baking powder	2 eggs
1 teaspoon salt	1/2 cup brandy
2 cups butter	1/4 cup sugar
1 1/2 cups sugar	1 tablespoon cinnamon

In a medium bowl sift together the flour, baking powder, and salt. In a large bowl cream together the butter, 1 1/2 cups of sugar, and anise seed. Beat the eggs until light and fluffy, and add to the creamed mixture. Add the flour mixture and the brandy, using only enough brandy to make a stiff dough. Mix until well blended. Knead slightly, and roll to 1/4-inch thickness. Combine 1/4 cup of sugar and the cinnamon, and dust the pastry with the mixture. Cut into shapes and place on a greased cookie sheet. Bake in a 350° oven for 10 minutes, or until lightly browned.

Makes 5 dozen.

Mary Ellis—Albuquerque, New Mexico

Nova Scotia Scones

2 cups all-purpose flour
2 teaspoons baking powder
1/2 teaspoon baking soda
1/2 teaspoon nutmeg
1/2 teaspoon salt
1/2 cup butter

1 cup raisins
2 tablespoons sugar
1 egg, separated
3/4 cup buttermilk or plain yogurt
Sugar

In a large bowl combine the flour, baking powder, baking soda, nutmeg, and salt. Mix well. Add the butter and cut into the dry ingredients with a pastry blender until the mixture resembles fine granules. Add the raisins and sugar, and toss well. Add the egg yolk to the buttermilk and whisk with a fork to blend. Pour the egg mixture over the flour mixture and stir with a fork until a soft dough forms. Turn the dough out onto a lightly floured surface and knead well. Cut the dough in half and knead each half briefly into a ball. Turn smooth side up and pat into 6-inch circles. Place on a cookie sheet. Score 6 wedges in the dough, but do not separate the wedges.

In a small bowl beat the egg white with a fork just until broken up. Brush the scones with the egg white and sprinkle with sugar. Bake in a 375° oven for 18 to 22 minutes.

These are great with marmalade.

Variations: You may experiment with cinnamon, blueberries, currants, raspberries, etc.
Serves 6.

Margaret Adams—Chicago, Illinois

Best Marble Squares

1 8-ounce package cream cheese
1/3 cup sugar
1 egg
1/2 cup margarine
1/4 cup water
1 1/2 ounces unsweetened chocolate
2 cups all-purpose flour

2 cups sugar
2 eggs
1/2 cup sour cream
1 teaspoon baking soda
1 teaspoon salt
6 ounces chocolate chips

Grease an 11 x 16-inch pan. In a large bowl combine the cream cheese, 1/3 cup of sugar, and 1 egg. Mix well. In a saucepan combine the margarine, water, and unsweetened chocolate, and bring to a boil. Remove from the heat. In a separate bowl combine the flour and remaining sugar. Stir into the chocolate mixture. Add the 2 eggs, sour cream, baking soda, and salt. Mix well. Pour into the prepared pan. Spoon the cheese mixture over the batter. Cut through with a knife to give a marbled effect. Sprinkle with chocolate chips. Bake in a 375° oven for 25 to 30 minutes.

2 cups sugar
1/2 cup margarine

1/2 cup milk
2 cups unsweetened chocolate chips

In a saucepan combine the sugar, margarine, and milk. Bring the mixture to a boil. Remove from the heat and add the chocolate chips. Stir until the mixture starts to thicken. Spread on the squares while still warm.
Serves 12.

James Best—cast member

Ernest T. Bass Rock Bars

Cool, cut, and eat—or throw. Caution: will break
glass if hurled from twelve feet or less.

1/2 cup butter
1/4 cup plus 2 tablespoons sugar
1/4 cup plus 2 tablespoons brown sugar
1 teaspoon vanilla extract
1 egg

1 cup all-purpose flour
1/2 teaspoon baking soda
1/2 teaspoon salt
1/2 cup coarsely chopped walnuts
1 cup semisweet chocolate chips

Grease and flour a 9 x 13-inch pan. In a large bowl cream the butter, sugar, brown sugar, and vanilla. Beat in the egg. In a separate bowl sift together the flour, soda, and salt. Blend the dry ingredients into the creamed mixture, and add the nuts. Spread the batter into the prepared pan, and sprinkle chocolate chips over the top. Bake in a 375° oven for 1 minute, remove, and cut through with a knife to create a marbled effect. Return to the oven and bake for 13 to 16 minutes or until golden brown.

Serves 12.

Bill Flynn—High Point, North Carolina

Bride and joy

Pitt's Maple Road Walnut Bars

A Christmas favorite you'll adore.

1 egg
1/2 cup sugar
1/3 cup butter, melted
1/2 cup self-rising flour

1 teaspoon maple flavoring
1 cup English walnuts, coarsely broken
1/2 cup chopped raisins

Grease an 8-inch square pan. In a large bowl beat the egg. Add the sugar and blend well. Add the melted butter, flour, maple flavoring, walnuts, and raisins. Mix until well blended. Spread evenly in the prepared pan. Bake in a 350° oven for 30 minutes. Cool in the pan. Cut into squares with a very sharp knife.

Makes 16 large or 20 small squares.

Eudora Garrison—Charlotte, North Carolina

Bullet Brownies

Be sure to eat them one at a time.

1 cup margarine
2 cups sugar
4 tablespoons cocoa
4 eggs, beaten

1¼ cups all-purpose flour
1 teaspoon vanilla extract
½ cup chopped nuts

Grease a 9-inch square pan, and dust with cocoa. In a saucepan melt the margarine. Add the sugar and cocoa, and blend well. Remove from the heat and add the remaining ingredients. Pour into the prepared pan. Bake in a 325° oven for 20 to 25 minutes.

These freeze well.

Serves 9.

Tina Muncy—Clarksville, Arkansas

Real (Not out of a Bottle) Blondies

Even better than reading Moon Mullins.

2 cups dark brown sugar
⅔ cup butter
2 teaspoons vanilla extract
2 eggs
2 cups all-purpose flour

1 teaspoon baking powder
¼ teaspoon baking soda
1 teaspoon salt
1 cup semisweet chocolate chips
1 cup chopped walnuts (or pecans)

Grease a 9 x 13-inch square baking pan. In a large bowl cream together the brown sugar and butter. Add the vanilla and eggs, and blend well. In a separate bowl sift together the flour, baking powder, baking soda, and salt. Fold in the chocolate chips and walnuts. Pour the batter into the prepared pan. Bake in a 350° oven for 20 to 30 minutes, or until a fork inserted in the center comes out fairly clean. Cool and cut.

Serves 12.

Jane Lambert—Greensboro, North Carolina

Goober Says Haystacks

'Nuff said.

1 12-ounce package butterscotch chips
1 12-ounce package semisweet chocolate chips

1 12-ounce package Chinese chow mein noodles

In a large saucepan over low heat, melt the butterscotch and chocolate chips. Add the chow mein noodles, coating well. Spoon onto waxed paper and chill until firm.

Makes 3 to 4 dozen.

Beverly Meyer—Nashville, Tennessee

Leon's Christmas Fudge

Leon—that's Noel spelled backwards, you know.

2 cups sugar
3 tablespoons cocoa
Dash salt
1/2 cup light corn syrup

1/2 cup Milnot (evaporated milk substitute)
1 teaspoon vanilla extract
2 tablespoons butter

Butter a glass pan. In a heavy pan combine the sugar, cocoa, salt, syrup, and Milnot. Cook, stirring constantly, to the soft ball stage. Add the vanilla and butter. Cool for a few minutes. When you can put your hand on the bottom of the pan, it is cool enough to continue. Beat the fudge until it turns a dull color and pour into the prepared pan.

Serves 6.

Pearl Harrison—Houston, Texas

Thelma Lou's Cashewless Fudge

No nuts allowed.

2 cups sugar
1 cup milk
4 tablespoons cocoa

1 tablespoon butter
Pinch salt
1 teaspoon vanilla extract

Grease a cookie sheet. In a saucepan combine the sugar, milk, and cocoa. Cook to the soft ball stage, and then stir in the remaining ingredients. Pour onto the prepared cookie sheet and allow to harden. Cut into squares.

Serves 8.

Grandma Greaves—Houston, Texas

BARNEY: (To Andy) Want some fudge? A man's had fudge every Tuesday night for years—you don't kick the habit just like that.

Thelma Lou's Cashew Fudge

Delicious—TV or not TV.

1/2 cup butter or margarine	1 3/4 to 2 cups sifted confectioners' sugar
1 cup packed brown sugar	1 cup cashews
1/4 cup milk	

Grease a 9-inch square pan. In a saucepan melt the butter and add the brown sugar. Cook over low heat for 2 minutes, stirring constantly. Add the milk and continue cooking, stirring until the mixture boils. Remove from the heat and allow to cool.

Gradually add the confectioners' sugar until the mixture is of fudge consistency. Add the nuts. Spread in the prepared pan and cool.

Makes 36 pieces.

Fudge lover

BARNEY: Thelma Lou and I have always had a standing date on Tuesday nights. Every Tuesday night for as long as I can remember we're setting on that couch, a pan of cashew fudge between us, watching that doctor show on TV.

Johnny Paul Jason's Pralines

2 cups brown sugar
1 cup sugar
1/8 teaspoon baking soda
2 tablespoons light corn syrup
1/2 cup water

3/4 can (14-ounce size) sweetened
  condensed milk
12 large marshmallows
1 quart pecan halves

In a saucepan combine all of the ingredients except the marshmallows and pecan halves. Cook until a small amount of the mixture forms a soft ball when dropped in cold water. Stir to prevent burning. Add the marshmallows and stir until melted. Remove from the heat and add the pecans. Beat until the mixture loses some of its gloss. Place waxed paper over cloth and drop the pralines by the spoonful onto the paper.

Makes 3 dozen.

Keith Thibodeaux—cast member

Floyd's Fiddle-Faddle

Fun fixin's for the whole crew.

8 cups popped popcorn (or 1 bag
  microwave corn)
1/2 cup pecan halves
1 3-ounce package sliced almonds

1/2 cup butter or margarine
1/2 cup firmly packed light brown sugar
1/2 teaspoon salt (or 1 teaspoon salt for
  unsalted corn)

Place the popcorn in a large bowl and set aside. Place the pecans and almonds on a large cookie sheet. Toast in a 350° oven for 10 minutes to make crisp.

In a saucepan combine the butter, sugar, and salt, and melt but do not boil. Stir briskly to blend well. Remove the nuts from the oven and add to the popcorn. Pour the butter mixture over the popcorn mixture, and stir with a large spoon until well coated. Spread out as thinly as possible onto a cookie sheet and return to the oven for 10 minutes. Remove from the oven and cool slightly. Remove from the pan with a spatula. It will continue to get crisp as it cools. Serve within a few hours, as it does not keep well.

Serves 6.

Ann Clark—Charlotte, North Carolina

Mistletoe mischief

Pearson's Peppermints

1 pound brown sugar
2 tablespoons vinegar
1/2 cup water

1/2 cup light corn syrup
1/4 teaspoon peppermint oil

Grease 2 cookie sheets. In a saucepan combine the brown sugar, vinegar, water, and corn syrup. Cook until the mixture forms a hard ball when dropped into cold water. Add the peppermint oil. Divide the mixture between the pans, and as soon as you can handle the candy, pull the candy on one pan like taffy until it is cream colored. Place on the dark candy in a zigzag pattern, and roll into thin sticks. Cut and place on waxed paper.

Grandma Greaves—Houston, Texas

Grand Caramel Corn

A box office smash! Rates four clovers.

5 quarts popped corn (2 to 3 bags
    microwave corn)
2 cups packed brown sugar
1 cup butter or margarine

1/2 cup light corn syrup
1 teaspoon baking soda
1 teaspoon vanilla extract
1 teaspoon salt

Spread the popcorn on baking sheets and set aside. In a large saucepan combine the brown sugar, butter, and corn syrup. Boil for 5 minutes, and remove from the heat. Add the baking soda, vanilla, and salt. Stir thoroughly. The mixture will "foam up." Pour over the popped corn and mix well. Bake in a 250° oven for 40 minutes. Stir every 15 minutes.

Makes 5 quarts.

Freida Crawley—Nashville, Tennessee

Mrs. Moore's Divinity

3 cups sugar
1/2 cup light corn syrup
I cup water

2 egg whites
1 to 1 1/2 cups black walnuts (these are a
   must)

In a saucepan combine the sugar, corn syrup, and water. Mix until the sugar is completely dissolved. Cook over medium heat, simmering slowly but not stirring, until a small amount "clanks" on the side of a cup when tried in cold water (254° on a candy thermometer). The trial amount must be brittle, not soft as with fudge. Remove from the heat without stirring. Beat the egg whites until stiff, but not dry. Slowly pour the syrup over the egg whites, beating constantly as you pour in a thin, slow stream. Continue beating until it begins to hold shape, and just before it sets up, add the walnuts and quickly stir until mixed. Drop quickly from the end of a teaspoon, pushing off with a blunt knife or another spoon, onto a hard surface covered with waxed paper or foil. Allow to cool completely and become firm, then store in a covered container.

Makes 5 to 6 dozen pieces of divinity.

Eudora Garrison—Charlotte, North Carolina

Peanut Patties Pyle

Sweet and nutty—just like Gomer and Goober.

2 1/2 cups sugar
2/3 cup light corn syrup
1 cup milk
2 1/2 cups raw peanuts

4 teaspoons margarine
Few drops red food coloring
1 cup confectioners' sugar

In a large pan combine the sugar, corn syrup, milk, and peanuts. Cook slowly until the mixture forms a soft ball. Remove from the heat and add the margarine, coloring, and confectioners' sugar. Stir until the mixture begins to thicken. Drop by big spoonfuls onto waxed paper.

Makes about 3 to 4 dozen.

Hazel Beck—North Little Rock, Arkansas

Clara Edwards Johnson

Though they can be keen rivals (notably in cooking, gardening, and courtship), Clara and Aunt Bee are the best of friends. They've known each other since their basketball-playing days at Sweetbriar Normal School.

Clara's pickles are without competition—especially from Aunt Bee. However, Aunt Bee can make a run for Clara's roses. And sooner or later, every potential beau knows that both ladies have a sporting chance at his affections.

Pickles, Relishes, and Sauces

Aunt Bee's Homemade Orange Marmalade

1 large grapefruit
3 lemons

3 large oranges
Sugar

Cut the fruit in halves and reserve the juice. Grind the peel and pulp with the medium-coarse blade of the meat chopper, and mix with the juice. Measure the juice and fruit mixture, and add 3 cups of water for every cup of fruit mixture. Set aside overnight.

The next day, boil the mixture for about 15 minutes. Set aside overnight.

The third day, measure the mixture and add 1 cup of sugar for each cup of mixture, plus 1 extra cup of sugar. Cook in at least 3 wide, heavy containers, boiling and skimming when necessary, until the mixture gels.

Makes 14 to 15 half-pint jars.

Mary Ketchin—Winnsboro, South Carolina

Cousin Toog's Bread and Butter Pickles

25 to 30 medium cucumbers
8 large onions
2 large bell peppers
1/2 cup pickling salt
5 cups vinegar

4 cups sugar
2 tablespoons mustard seed
1 teaspoon turmeric
1/2 teaspoon cloves

Wash the cucumbers and slice thin. Slice the onions, chop the peppers, and combine with the cucumber slices. Add the salt. Let the mixture stand for 3 hours, then drain.

In a large stock pot combine the remaining ingredients and bring to a boil. Add the drained cucumber mixture and heat thoroughly. Do not boil. Pack into sterilized jars while still hot, and seal.

Everett and Deane Ward Greenbaum—writer

Aunt Bee's Kerosene Cucumbers

These homemade pickles are popular everywhere from Oregon to Nova Scotia. They're delicious. Trust us. Really.

Cucumbers	6 teaspoons whole spices
1 bunch dill	6 lumps alum
6 hot peppers	1 quart cider vinegar
6 cloves garlic	2 quarts water
6 slices onion	1 cup salt

Wash and dry enough cucumbers for 6 sterilized 1-quart jars. In the bottom of each jar place a portion of the dill, 1 hot pepper, 1 clove of garlic, 1 slice of onion, 1 teaspoon of whole spices, a small lump of alum, and cucumbers. In a saucepan combine the vinegar, water, and salt. Let the mixture come to a rolling boil, then pour into the jars. Seal immediately.

Makes 6 quarts.

Alice and Jim Schwenke—Houston, Texas

Clara tries one of Aunt Bee's homemade pickles:
AUNT BEE: What do you think, Clara?
    CLARA: Oh, they're very nice, very nice indeed. They're quite pleasant and nice.
AUNT BEE: Really?
    CLARA: Oh, yes. Yes indeed. I wouldn't change them one single bit . . . except the brine might be just a touch too heavy.
AUNT BEE: Well, I was very careful . . .
    CLARA: . . . But that's the only thing. Maybe an extra sprig or two of parsley steeped in vinegar and possibly if you could get younger cucumbers, they wouldn't be so soft. Then drain them more and use fresher spices. But other than that, they're . . . quite nice. . . . Oh, you might try boiling the vinegar just two seconds more too. . . . But they're *nice*.

Island Cucumbers in Vinegar

1 cup vinegar	1/4 teaspoon salt
2 tablespoons water	1/4 teaspoon pepper
3 tablespoons sugar	Cucumbers

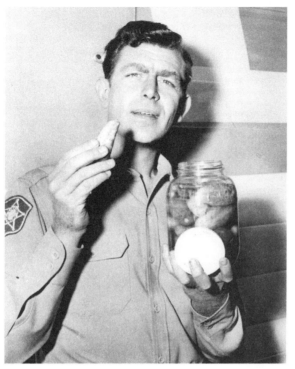

"Learn to love 'em."

In a saucepan combine the vinegar, water, sugar, salt, and pepper. Bring to a boil. Let the mixture cool. Place in a glass jar with a lid, and chill in the refrigerator.

An hour before using, cut cucumbers into very thin slices (but do not peel) and add to the vinegar solution. Cover and refrigerate.

Tonya Hamel—Greensboro, North Carolina

Aunt Bee brings some of her homemade pickles to the courthouse:

ANDY: Well, that certainly is a wonderful surprise. Looka there, Barney, Aunt Bee's brought us some of her homemade pickles.

BARNEY: I see. Sure is wonderful. You really shouldn't have, Aunt Bee.

ANDY: That's right, Aunt Bee. You go to *way* yonder too much trouble to please us.

AUNT BEE: Oh, it's no trouble at all. There're plenty. I made eight quarts.

ANDY: Eight quarts? Oh-h, Aunt Bee made eight quarts . . . eight quarts.

AUNT BEE: So you can have some every day. Try one.

BARNEY: Oh, well, I had an awful big breakfast. I just stuffed myself something terrible.

Pickled Tink Red Cabbage

1 head red cabbage	Salt
1 quart white vinegar	

Grate, rinse, and drain the cabbage. In a pot combine the cabbage and vinegar. Turn the heat to high. Add salt. When the mixture starts to steam, turn the heat to medium. Cook covered for 30 to 45 minutes. It will be done when the cabbage has a soft texture. Drain the cabbage. Let the cabbage cool and place in a quart jar. Add the vinegar for storage.

Makes 1 quart.

Steven and Holly Yates—Nashville, Tennessee

Mrs. Wiley's Watermelon Rind

3 pounds watermelon rind	Whole cloves (small handful)
3 pounds sugar	3 to 4 sticks cinnamon
1 pint vinegar	1 tablespoon whole allspice

Peel the green outer rind from the watermelon rind. Some, but very little, pink should be left. In a saucepan cover the rind with cold water and bring to a boil. Reduce the heat and simmer until the rind is tender enough to pierce easily with a fork.

While the rind is cooking, combine the remaining ingredients and cook until the rind is done. Drain the rind and soak in cold water, pouring off the water and replacing it several times. When cool, drain and cover with ice cubes. After the rind is thoroughly chilled, combine the rind and the syrup in a large saucepan and bring to a boil. Reduce the heat and simmer for 45 minutes. Put in jars while still hot. The spices can be put in the jars with the rind.

Makes 6 to 8 pints.

What do you call people who've eaten too many pickles?
ANDY: Just gluttons, gluttons, gluttons, gluttons, glut-tons!

Cousin Leda's Banana Chutney

6 bananas	1 tablespoon salt
1 cup minced onion	1 teaspoon ground ginger
1 cup raisins	1 teaspoon nutmeg
1 cup minced tart apples	1 teaspoon cayenne pepper
1 cup apple cider vinegar	$1/3$ cup lemon juice
2 cups sugar	3 cloves garlic, minced

Peel and mash the bananas. In a large casserole dish combine all of the ingredients. Bake in a 350° oven for about 2 hours, stirring occasionally. When thickened, ladle into sterilized jars and seal.

Makes about 2 pints.

Everett and Deane Ward Greenbaum—writer

How were those pickles?
BARNEY: No mistake about it—that's a pickle.
ANDY: Yeah, boy.

Lydia's Chitchat Chili Sauce

Talk of the town.

24 ripe tomatoes	3 teaspoons salt
10 onions	1 teaspoon cinnamon
2 green peppers	1 teaspoon cloves
2 cups firmly packed brown sugar	1 teaspoon allspice
1 pint vinegar	1 teaspoon nutmeg

Plunge the tomatoes in boiling water, and remove the skins. Cut the tomatoes into small pieces. Finely chop the onions and peppers. In a large saucepan combine all of the ingredients, and cook until thick. Pour into sterilized jars and seal, or freeze in small batches.

Clara Greaves—Houston, Texas

Maple Road Syrup

1 cup sugar
1 cup firmly packed brown sugar

1 cup water
Maple flavoring

In a saucepan combine the sugar, brown sugar, and water, and bring to a boil. Stir until the sugars are dissolved. Add maple flavoring to taste.
   Makes about 1 cup.

Tara Concelman—Houston, Texas

Aunt Bee's cure for hiccups: Hold your breath and take five sips of water.
Floyd's hiccup cure: Inhale in front of an electric fan.

Andy Pasto Spread

Spread the word—it's gooood.

2 4-ounce cans mushroom stems and
   pieces, drained and finely chopped
1 14-ounce can artichoke hearts, drained
   and finely chopped
1 10-ounce jar pimento-stuffed olives,
   drained and finely chopped
1 6-ounce can ripe olives, drained and
   finely chopped
1/4 cup chopped green pepper
1/4 cup chopped celery

1 cup vinegar
1/2 cup olive oil
1/4 cup minced onion
2 1/2 teaspoons Italian seasoning
1 teaspoon onion salt
1 teaspoon salt
1 teaspoon seasoned salt
1 teaspoon garlic salt
1 teaspoon sugar
1 teaspoon cracked black pepper

In a large bowl combine the mushrooms, artichoke hearts, olives, green pepper, and celery. In a saucepan combine the remaining ingredients and bring to a boil. Pour the dressing over the vegetables, and place the mixture in a large jar with a tight-fitting lid. Shake the jar, and refrigerate overnight.
   Best when served with crackers before leg o' lamb dinner prepared by Aunt Bee.

Bill Flynn—High Point, North Carolina

Barbershop Barbecue Sauce

A prince of a tonic for your favorite meats.

2 8-ounce bottles Worcestershire sauce
2 12-ounce bottles chili sauce
2 16-ounce bottles catsup
1 onion, chopped

Garlic salt to taste
1/2 cup butter
Bay leaves

In a saucepan combine all of the ingredients, and simmer for as long as possible. Store in a container with a tight-fitting lid.

Sherry Hyatt—Kingsport, Tennessee

Andy's Red Hot Applesauce

7 or 8 medium Granny Smith apples
Water

1/2 cup red hots
3 tablespoons sugar

Peel and core the apples and chop into large chunks. Place in a saucepan and cover almost completely with water. Cover the pan. Bring to a simmer over medium heat. Reduce the heat and simmer for 20 minutes or until the apples are tender, stirring occasionally. Remove from the heat and spoon out as much water as possible. Add the red hots and sugar, and stir until dissolved. Cover and refrigerate.

Serves 6.

Mary Clark—Nashville, Tennessee

Crowley's Cranberries

1 12-ounce bag cranberries
1 1/2 cups sugar

1/2 cup water

Place the cranberries in a shallow baking dish. Sprinkle with sugar and add water to cover. Bake in a 350° oven for 45 minutes to 1 hour, until the cranberries pop and form their own glaze.

Serve warm.

Serves 4.

Bill and LuAnne Dugan—Wynne, Arkansas

Hollister Hollandaise

The perfect accompaniment.

2 tablespoons butter
1 tablespoon all-purpose flour
Boiling water
Juice of 1 lemon

Salt to taste
Dash cayenne
Dash onion salt
2 egg yolks, beaten

In the top of a double boiler over simmering water, melt the butter, and stir in the flour until blended. Add enough hot water to make a fairly thick sauce, stirring and cooking until smooth. Add the lemon juice, salt, cayenne, and onion salt. Add the egg yolks, stirring and cooking until smooth and thick. This can be kept in the top of a double boiler for 30 minutes or more without separating. Reheat before serving, of course. A bit more butter or hot water may be added if the sauce is too thick.

Serves 4 to 6.

Eudora Garrison—Charlotte, North Carolina

Otis Campbell's Favorite Red Eye Gravy

So good you'll want to drink it.

Ham meat doesn't fry much, so put grease in with it when you fry it. Take the meat out and pour the grease in a bowl. Sprinkle sugar on the hot frying pan. Pour about ½ cup of water on the skillet. It'll fry like lightning, so just cook it until it's hot, about 1 minute. Pour it over the grease in the bowl and that's when you get your red.

Makes about 1 cup.

Lois Rogers—Readyville, Tennessee

Index

Acknowledgments

Eating may speak louder than words. Nevertheless, a whole lot of folks helped make this cookbook rise to something beyond a half-baked idea, and we want to thank them.

The brilliant work done by the cast and crew of *The Andy Griffith Show* has been our inspiration. Several of the cast also gave us permission to use photographs of themselves as they appeared in Mayberry. We are grateful to be able to include photographs of their characters in this book.

In addition, many of the cast and crew have joined outstanding cooks from across the country in providing favorite recipes for this cookbook. Attributions for their offerings accompany their recipes. We're grateful to everyone who submitted recipes.

We've spiced up the cookbook with dialogue from the show and with facts about Mayberry foods and eating. For this we express our gratitude and admiration for the show's talented writers. Their words are our "awe spice."

We also thank artist Mike Johnson for his drawing of the Snappy Lunch in Mount Airy, North Carolina, and Snappy Lunch owner Charles Dowell for his enthusiastic participation.

Everyone at Rutledge Hill Press for the 1991 edition was supportive of our work on this cookbook. Editors Ron Pitkin and Larry Stone believed in the idea, and Julie Pitkin added invaluable expertise as editor of the recipes.

We thank editor Ty Powers for his expertise in overseeing the production of this new hardcover edition for Nelson Books. We're grateful to graphic designer Lori Lynch and cover designer Jamie DeBruyn for beautifully capturing the feel of Mayberry with this edition's updated design. We appreciate Rhonda Lowry and Lauren Schneider for their precise proofreading and indexing skills. Our special thanks also to Stephanie Newton, director of backlist development, for conceiving and championing this new edition, and to senior sales director Damon Reiss for his enthusiastic support.

Finally, we want to thank from the bottom of our hearts (and the tops of our stomachs) those who have prepared delicious meals and fed these two hungry Goobers over the years. While we're pretty good dishwashers and can fashion peanut butter and jelly sandwiches with the best of them, we're basically lost in the kitchen without a lot of help. Our main talent is simply recognizing good food and eating it.

For the record, those who have prepared most of Ken's meals are: Grandma Beck, Grandma Rogers, Hazel (Mama) Beck, and his very patient wife, Wendy. Jim has become the Goober he is primarily through the recipes and cooking of Tonya (Gramma) Hamel, Nancy (Mom) Clark, and his supportive and understanding wife, Mary, who was an especially big help with suggestions for menus.

We thank you all!

All done—except for cleaning a few dishes

Food to Watch

Members of *The Andy Griffith Show* Rerun Watchers Club agree that food is a big part of Mayberry. Among the names they've chosen for their chapters are more than a hundred that make reference to food and eating, including the following:

The 79¢ Blue Plate Special Over at the Diner	Columbus, GA
$1.75	Lawrenceville, GA
150 Pounds of Beef	Topeka, KS
"Ain't We Picking Our Peaches Before They're Fuzzed Up Good?"	Harrison, OH
"Amazing! Only This Morning He Didn't Know Which Side to Butter His Bread On, and a Few Hours Later He's a Genius! It Could Only Happen in America."	Walhalla, SC
Ange and Barn's Fancy Eatin' Place	Brazil, IN
"Aunt Bee, She'll Brang You Some Chicken an' Dumplin's an' Sweet Tater Pie for Supper"	Oconomowoc, WI/Inman, SC
Aunt Bee's Canton Palace	Smyrna, TN
Aunt Bee's Home Cooking	Cheviot, OH
Aunt Bee's Pickle Pinchers	Rescue, CA
Aunt Bee's Pickles	Perry, GA
Aunt Bee's Pickles . . . Learn to Love 'Em	Denton, NC
"Bad Old Home Pickles"	Kingston Springs, TN
"Barney, You're Gassed!"	Cedarburg, WI
Barney's Front Porch Cider Sippers and Car Counters	Jonesborough, TN
Bendlemight's Porchside Cider Sippers	Nickel Ranch, CA
Bluebird Diner	High Point, NC
"'Bout to Pop"	Grayson, GA
"Bread!"	Savannah, GA
Cashew Fudge	Dyersburg, TN
"Charlene, Let Your Old Paw Have That Heel"	Austin, TX
A Cherry for Thelma Lou	Decatur, IL
"Chewin' Tar Is Good for Your Teeth"	Varysburg, NY
Colonel Harvey's Elixir	Jacksonville, FL

"Clock in the Stomach"	Columbus, IN
"Could Ya Reach My Fork?"	Fayetteville, AR
County Line Café	Jonesboro, AR
Corned Beef and Cabbage at the Diner on Tuesdays	West Columbia, SC
"Cream Puff"	Greenville, SC
The Diner	Plymouth, IN
"Don't Give Him My Mr. Cookie Bar, Andy"	Lewiston, ME
"Don't Pick Your Peaches 'til They're All Fuzzed Up"	Madison, IN
"Drink Hard Cider and Holler 'Flinch'"	Ramseur, NC
Escargots et Cerveaux du Boeuf	Alexander City, AL
"Fellas Don't Light Candles When They're Eatin' by Themselves"	Midland, TX
Fish Muddle	Yukon, OR
Foley's Market	Farmington, MO
"Food and Water for My Men and Horses!"	Hokes Bluff, AL
From Miracle Salve to Kerosene Cucumbers	Celina, OH
"Get a Bottle of Pop"	Gadsden, AL
"Gluttons, Gluttons, Glut-tons"	Las Vegas, NV
"Gravy Is No Joke, No Siree"	Rochester, IL
Gravy Sandwich	Tupelo, MS
"Great Beans, Aunt Bee!"	Nashville, TN
"Half Mad with Thirst"	Denver, CO
"Hearty-Eatin' Men and Beautiful, Delicate Women"	Tuscaloosa, AL
"Hit Her with a Leg of Lamb!"	Simpsonville, SC
"Hooked Like a Starving Catfish"	Huntsville, TX
Hoot Owl Pie	Troy, AL
The Huckleberry Smash Club	Valley City, ND
"I Came to Fill My Vase"	Waxhaw, NC
"I Can Take a Bossy Mouth, but I Ain't About to Be Beat to Death with No Spoon"	Oxnard, CA
"I Do that So's I Can Talk Whilst I Eat"	Port Neches, TX
"I Don't Chew My Cabbage Twice"	Cincinnati, OH/Phillipsburg, NJ
"I Got a Hobby—Drinking"	Normal, IL
"I Have a Fortune of Meat in There"	Denver, CO
"I Passed It! I Didn't Heave It!"	Nashville, TN
"I Swallowed My Gum"	Ackley, IA
"I Think I've Heard Just About Enough About That Tomato"	Tuscola, IL

"Icka Backa, Soda Cracker, Icka Backa Boo"	Northfield, MN
"Just Another Place at the Table for Friday Night Supper"	Richfield, WI
"Just Had to Have an Apple"	Vidalia, LA
Kerosene Cucumbers	Asheville, NC
"Learn to Love 'Em"	Charlotte, NC
"Leg of Lamb, Andy's Favorite Dish"	Portsmouth, OH
Licorice Seeds	Cincinnati, OH
"Little Sweet Tea and Spicy Talk"	Spokane, WA
The Malcolm Tucker Front Porch Apple Peelers	Carrington, ND
"Maud, Al! If Those Hamburgers Are Ruined, I Won't Be Responsible!"	Fort Wayne, IN
The Mayberry Chef	Evans, PA
Mayberry Cider Sippers	Bridgeport, CA
The Mayberry Donut Shop	Cincinnati, OH/Cyberspace
The Mayberry Porch-Rocking Apple Peelers	Roanoke, VA
Mayberry Supper Club	Orlando, FL
"Meat!"	Ames, IA
Morrison Sisters Elixir	Eden, NC
Mr. Cookie Bar	Covington, TN
Mt. Pilot Supper Club	Cincinnati, OH
"Mulberry Squeezin's"	Greer, SC
Murphy's House of the Nine Flavors	Keyser, WV
Myers Lake Bait Shop	Perrysburg, OH
Nectarine Crush	Rock Hill, SC
"No Coffee Tea or Punch Thank You"	Timmonsville, SC
"No More Peanut Butter and Jelly Sandwiches"	Montevallo, AL
"Now That's a Pickle"	Roanoke, VA
"Oh, Morelli's!"	Waco, TX
"Oh, They Twang My Buds!"	Niwot, CO
Old Aunt Maria's Café	Moss Point, MS
"Operation Pickle Switch"	Creston, OH
Opie and Aunt Bee and a Coaster Wagon and a Pack of Yappin' Dogs	Williston, FL
"Otis, Otis Campbell, Where Did You Get the Liquor?"	Great Bend, KS
"Pearly Onions Twang My Buds"	Leavenworth, KS
Pepperelli Pizza	Fayetteville, NC
The Pounded Steak	Hamilton, OH

"A Sandwich Sure Tastes Better with Milk"	Fort Smith, AR
The Secret Ingredient: Oregano	Huntington, WV
Singin' "Eating Goober Peas" with Ernest T.	Fillmore, IN
Snails and Brains Dinner Club	Galveston, IN
The Snappy Lunch	Morehead City, NC
Starbricks	Nelsonville, OH
"Still Ugly, Single, and Pitting Prunes"	Casey, IL
Syrup and Biscuits	Headland, AL
"Taters!"	Indianapolis, IN
"They Were Just Pickled Tink to See Me"	Kingsport, TN
"This Cider's Turned Hard"	Conyers, GA/Calumet City, IL
Tomato Catchers Club	Lecanto, FL
West Indian Licorice Mocha Delight	Lexington, TN
"What Do You Know, Spaghetti!"	Mount Pleasant, PA
"What You Need Is More Sauce!"	Haines, AK
"Where Did You Hide the Liquor, Otis?"	Southport, NC
"Why'd You Throw a Tomato at Me, Barney?"	Avon, CT
"Wild Pheasant, Perhaps the Most Difficult Species of All to Ensnare"	Greencastle, IN

If you would like more information about what's cooking in Mayberry, you can write *The Andy Griffith Show* Rerun Watchers Club the old-fashioned way at:

TAGSRWC
118 16th Avenue South
Suite 4, PMB 146
Nashville, TN 37203–3100

Or you can find TAGSRWC online at www.tagsrwc.com and www.facebook.com/tagsrwc.